THIRD EDITION

CSS
Pocket Reference

Eric A. Meyer

O'REILLY®

Beijing · Cambridge · Farnham · Köln · Paris · Sebastopol · Taipei · Tokyo

CSS™ Pocket Reference, Third Edition

by Eric A. Meyer

Copyright © 2008 O'Reilly Media, Inc. All rights reserved.
Originally printed in Canada. ISBN-10: 0-596-51505-7, ISBN-13: 978-0-596-51505-8

Published by O'Reilly Media, Inc., 1005 Gravenstein Highway North, Sebastopol, CA 95472.

O'Reilly books may be purchased for educational, business, or sales promotional use. Online editions are also available for most titles (safari.oreilly.com). For more information, contact our corporate/ institutional sales department: (800) 998-9938 or *corporate@oreilly.com*.

Editor: Tatiana Apandi	**Cover Designer:** Karen Montgomery
Production Editor: Loranah Dimant	**Interior Designer:** David Futato
Proofreader: Loranah Dimant	**Illustrator:** Jessamyn Read
Indexer: Reg Aubry	

Printing History:

May 2001:	First Edition.
July 2004:	Second Edition.
October 2007:	Third Edition.

First Indian Reprint: June 2009

ISBN 10: 81-8404-716-9
ISBN 13: 978-81-8404-716-5

Nutshell Handbook, the Nutshell Handbook logo, and the O'Reilly logo are registered trademarks of O'Reilly Media, Inc. *The Pocket Reference* series designations, *CSS Pocket Reference*, Third Edition, the image of salmon, and related trade dress are trademarks of O'Reilly Media, Inc.

Many of the designations used by manufacturers and sellers to distinguish their products are claimed as trademarks. Where those designations appear in this book, and O'Reilly Media, Inc. was aware of a trademark claim, the designations have been printed in caps or initial caps.

Published by **Shroff Publishers and Distributors Pvt. Ltd.** C-103, MIDC, TTC Industrial Area, Pawane, Navi Mumbai 400 705, Tel: (91 22) 4158 4158, Fax: 4158 4141, e-mail: spdorders@shroffpublishers.com. Printed at Rose Fine Art, Mumbai.

Contents

CSS Pocket Reference

Cascading Style Sheets (CSS) is the W3C standard for the visual presentation of web pages (although it can be used in other settings as well). After a short introduction to the key concepts of CSS, this pocket reference provides an alphabetical reference to all CSS2.1 selectors, followed by an alphabetical reference to all CSS2.1 properties.

Conventions Used in This Book

The following typographical conventions are used in this book:

Italic

Used to indicate new terms, URLs, filenames, file extensions, directories, commands and options, and program names. For example, a path in the filesystem will appear as *C:\windows\system*.

Constant width

Used to show the contents of files or the output from commands.

For more information, visit O'Reilly's web site for this book, where examples, errata, and any plans for future editions are listed:

http://www.oreilly.com/catalog/9780596515058

Safari® Books Online

When you see a Safari® Books Online icon on the cover of your favorite technology book, that means the book is available online through the O'Reilly Network Safari Bookshelf.

Safari offers a solution that's better than e-books. It's a virtual library that lets you easily search thousands of top tech books, cut and paste code samples, download chapters, and find quick answers when you need the most accurate, current information. Try it for free at *http://safari.oreilly.com*.

Adding Styles to HTML and XHTML

Styles can be applied to documents in three distinct ways, as discussed in the following sections.

Inline Styles

In HTML and XHTML, style information can be specified for an individual element via the style attribute. The value of a style attribute is a declaration block (see the upcoming section "Rule Structure") without the curly braces:

```
<p style="color: red; background: yellow;">Look out!
This text is alarmingly presented!</p>
```

Note that, as of this writing, a full style sheet cannot be placed into a style attribute. Only the content of a single declaration block can be used as a style attribute value. For example, it is not possible to place hover styles (using :hover) in a style attribute, nor can one use @import in this context.

Although typical XML document languages (e.g., XHTML 1.0, XHTML 1.1, and SVG) support the style attribute, it is unlikely that all XML languages will support a similar capability. Due to this and the fact that it encourages poor authoring practices, authors are generally discouraged from using the style attribute.

Embedded Style Sheets

A style sheet can be embedded at the top of an HTML or XHTML document using the style element, which must appear within the head element:

```
<html><head><title>Stylin'!</title>
<style type="text/css">
h1 {color: purple;}
p {font-size: smaller; color: gray;}
</style>
</head>
    ...
</html>
```

XML languages may or may not provide an equivalent capability; always check the language DTD to be certain.

External Style Sheets

Styles can be listed in a separate file. The primary advantage to a separate file is that by collecting commonly used styles in a single file, all pages using that style sheet can be updated by editing a single style sheet. Another key advantage is that external style sheets are cached, which can help reduce bandwidth usage. An external style sheet can be referenced in one of the following three ways:

@import directive

One or more @import directives can be placed at the beginning of any style sheet. For HTML and XHTML documents, this would be done within an embedded style sheet:

```
<head>
<title>My Document</title>
<style type="text/css">
@import url(site.css);
@import url(navbar.css);
@import url(footer.css);
body {background: yellow;}
</style>
</head>
```

Note that @import directives can appear at the top (and, according to the specification, *only* at the top) of any style sheet. Thus, one style sheet could import another, which in turn would import a third.

link element

In HTML and XHTML documents, the link element can be used to associate a style sheet with a document. Multiple link elements are permitted. The media attribute can be used to restrict a style sheet to one or more media:

```
<head>
<title>A Document</title>
<link rel="stylesheet" type="text/css" href="basic.css"
  media="all">
<link rel="stylesheet" type="text/css" href="web.css"
  media="screen">
<link rel="stylesheet" type="text/css" href="paper.css"
  media="print">
</head>
```

It is also possible to link to alternate style sheets. If alternate style sheets are supplied, it is up to the user agent (or the author) to provide a means for the user to select one of the alternates:

```
<head>
<title>A Document</title>
<link rel="stylesheet" type="text/css" href="basic.css">
<link rel="alternate stylesheet" title="Classic"
type="text/css" href="oldschool.css">
<link rel="alternate stylesheet" title="Futuristic"
type="text/css" href="3000ad.css">
</head>
```

As of this writing, most or all known user agents load all linked style sheets, including the alternate style sheets, regardless of whether the user ever implements them. This can have implications for bandwidth use and server load.

xml-stylesheet processing instruction

In XML documents (such as XHTML documents sent with a mime-type of "text/xml," "application/xml," or "application/xhtml+xml"), an xml-stylesheet processing instruction can be used to associate a style sheet with a document. Any xml-stylesheet processing instructions must be placed in the prolog of an XML document. Multiple xml-stylesheet processing instructions are permitted. The media pseudoattribute can be used to restrict a style sheet to one or more forms of media:

```
<?xml-stylesheet type="text/css" href="basic.css"
  media="all"?>
<?xml-stylesheet type="text/css" href="web.css"
  media="screen"?>
<?xml-stylesheet type="text/css" href="paper.css"
  media="print"?>
```

It is also possible to link to alternate style sheets with the xml-stylesheet processing instruction:

```
<?xml-stylesheet type="text/css" href="basic.css"?>
<?xml-stylesheet alternate="yes" title="Classic"
  type="text/css" href="oldschool.css"?>
<?xml-stylesheet alternate="yes" title="Futuristic"
  type="text/css" href="3000ad.css"?>
```

Rule Structure

A style sheet consists of one or more rules that describe how page elements should be presented. Every rule has two fundamental parts: the *selector* and the *declaration block*. Figure 1 illustrates the structure of a rule.

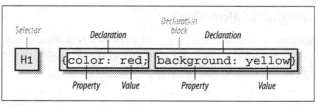

Figure 1. Rule structure

On the left side of the rule, we find the selector, which selects the parts of the document to which the rule should be applied. On the right side of the rule, we have the declaration block. A declaration block is made up of one or more *declarations*; each declaration is a combination of a CSS *property* and a *value* of that property.

The declaration block is always enclosed in curly braces. A declaration block can contain several declarations; each declaration must be terminated with a semicolon (;). The exception is the final declaration in a declaration block, for which the semicolon is optional.

Each property, which represents a particular stylistic parameter, is separated from its value by a colon (:). Property names in CSS are not case-sensitive. Legal values for a property are defined by the property description. The "Property Reference" section, later in this book, provides details on acceptable values for CSS properties.

Style Precedence

A single HTML or XHTML document can import and link to multiple external style sheets, contain one or more embedded style sheets, and make use of inline styles. In the process, it is quite possible that some rules will conflict with each other. CSS uses a mechanism called the *cascade* to resolve any such conflicts and arrive at a final set of styles to be applied to the document. Two key components of the cascade are *specificity* and *inheritance*.

Specificity Calculations

Specificity describes the weight of a selector and any declarations associated with it. The following table summarizes the components of specificity summation.

Selector type	Specificity
Universal selector Combinators	0,0,0,0
Element identifier Pseudo-element identifier	0,0,0,1
Class identifier Pseudo-class identifier Attribute identifier	0,0,1,0
ID identifier	0,1,0,0
Inline style attribute	1,0,0,0

Specificity values are cumulative; thus, a selector containing two element identifiers and a class identifier (e.g., div.aside p) has a specificity of 0,0,1,2. Specificity values are sorted in right-to-left precedence; thus, a selector containing 11 element identifiers (0,0,0,11) has a lower specificity than a selector containing just a single class identifier (0,0,1,0).

The !important directive gives a declaration more weight than nonimportant declarations. The declaration retains the specificity of its selectors and is used only in comparison with other important declarations.

Inheritance

The elements in a document form a tree-like hierarchy with the root element at the top and the rest of the document structure spreading out below it (which makes it look more like a tree root system, really). In an HTML document, the html element is at the top of the tree, with the head and body elements descending from it. The rest of the document structure descends from those elements. In such a structure, elements lower down in the tree are descendants of the ancestors, which are higher in the tree.

CSS uses the document tree for the mechanism of *inheritance*, in which a style applied to an element is inherited by its descendants. For example, if the body element is set to have a color of red, that value propagates down the document tree to the elements that descend from the body element. Inheritance is interrupted only by a style rule that applies directly to an element. Inherited values have no specificity at all (which is *not* the same as having zero specificity).

Note that some elements are not inherited. A property will always define whether it is inherited. Some examples of non-inherited properties are padding, border, margin, and background.

The Cascade

The cascade is how CSS resolves conflicts between styles; in other words, it is the mechanism by which a user agent decides, for example, what color to make an element when two different rules apply to it and each one tries to set a different color. The following steps constitute the cascade:

1. Find all declarations that contain a selector that matches a given element.

2. Sort by explicit weight all declarations applying to the element. Those rules marked !important are given greater weight than those that are not. Also, sort by origin all declarations applying to a given element. There are three origins: author, reader, and user agent. Under normal circumstances, the author's styles win out over the reader's styles. !important reader styles are stronger than any other styles, including !important author styles. Both author and reader styles override the user agent's default styles.

3. Sort by specificity all declarations applying to a given element. Those elements with a higher specificity have more weight than those with lower specificity.

4. Sort by order all declarations applying to a given element. The later a declaration appears in a style sheet or a document, the more weight it is given. Declarations that appear in an imported style sheet are considered to come before all declarations within the style sheet that imports them.

Element Classification

Broadly speaking, CSS groups elements into two types: *nonreplaced* and *replaced*. Although the types may seem rather abstract, there actually are some profound differences in how the two kinds of elements are presented. These differences are explored in detail in Chapter 7 of *CSS: The Definitive Guide*, Third Edition (O'Reilly).

Nonreplaced Elements

The majority of HTML and XHTML elements are *nonreplaced elements*, which means their content is presented by the user agent inside a box generated by the element itself. For example, `<span>hi there</span>` is a nonreplaced element, and the text hi there will be displayed by the user agent. Paragraphs, headings, table cells, lists, and almost everything else in HTML and XHTML are nonreplaced elements.

Replaced Elements

In contrast, *replaced elements* are those whose content is replaced by something not directly represented by document content. The most familiar XHTML example is the img element, which is replaced by an image file external to the document itself. In fact, img itself has no actual content, as we can see by considering a simple example:

```
<img src="howdy.gif" alt="Hi" />
```

There is no content contained in the element—only an element name and attributes. Only by replacing the element's lack of content with content found through other means (in this case, loading an external image specified by the src attribute) can the element have any presentation at all. Another example is the input element, which may be replaced with a radio button, checkbox, or text input box, depending on its type. Replaced elements also generate boxes in their display.

Element Display Roles

In addition to being replaced or not, there are two basic types of element display roles in CSS2: *block-level* and *inline-level*.

Block-Level

Block-level elements are those that generate an element box that (by default) fills its parent element's content area and cannot have other elements to its sides. In other words, block-level elements generate "breaks" before and after the element box. The most familiar block elements from HTML are p and div. Replaced elements can be block-level elements but usually are not.

List items are a special case of block-level elements. In addition to behaving in a manner consistent with other block elements, they generate a marker—typically a bullet for unordered lists or a number for ordered lists—which is "attached" to the element box. Except for the presence of this marker, list items are identical to other block elements.

Inline-Level Elements

Inline-level elements are those that generate an element box within a line of text and do not break up the flow of that line.

The best-known inline element is the a element in HTML and XHTML. Other examples are span and em. These elements do not generate a break before or after themselves, so they can appear within the content of another element without disrupting its display.

Note that although the CSS block and inline elements have a great deal in common with HTML and XHTML block- and inline-level elements, there is an important difference. In HTML and XHTML, block-level elements cannot descend from inline-level elements, whereas in CSS, there is no restriction on how display roles can be nested within each other.

Basic Visual Layout

CSS defines algorithms for laying out any element in a document. These algorithms form the underpinnings of visual presentation in CSS. There are two primary kinds of layout, each with very different behaviors: block-level and inline-level layout.

Block-Level Layout

A block-level box in CSS generates a rectangular box called the *element box*, which describes the amount of space occupied by an element. Figure 2 shows the various components of an element box. The following rules apply to an element box:

- The background of an element extends to the outer edge of the border, thus filling the content, padding, and border areas. If the border has any transparent portions (e.g., it is dotted or dashed), then the background will be visible in those portions.

- Only the margins, height, and width of an element box may be set to auto.

- Only margins can be given negative values.

- The padding and borders of the element box default to 0 (zero) and none, respectively.
- The property width defines only the width of the content area; any padding, borders, or margins are added to it. The same is true for height.

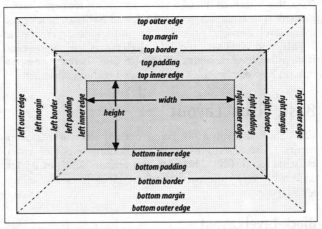

Figure 2. Box model details

Inline Layout

All inline elements have a line-height, which has a great deal to do with how the elements are displayed. The height of a line of text is determined by taking into account the following factors:

Anonymous text

Any string of characters not contained within an inline element. Thus, in the markup:

```
<p> I'm <em>so</em> happy!</p>
```

the sequences "I'm" and "happy!" are anonymous text. Note that the spaces are part of that text, as a space is a character like any other.

Em-box

The em-box defined in the given font; otherwise known as the character box. Actual glyphs can be taller or shorter than their em-boxes, as discussed in Chapter 5 of *CSS: The Definitive Guide*, Third Edition (O'Reilly). In CSS, the value of font-size determines the height of each em-box.

Content area

In nonreplaced elements, the content area can be the box described by the em-boxes of every character in the element, strung together, or else the box described by the character glyphs in the element. The CSS2.1 specification allows user agents to choose either. This text uses the em-box definition for simplicity's sake. In replaced elements, the content area is the intrinsic height of the element plus any margins, borders, or padding.

Leading

The leading is the difference between the values of font-size and line-height. Half this difference is applied to the top and half to the bottom of the content area. These additions to the content area are called, not surprisingly, half-leading. Leading is applied only to nonreplaced elements.

Inline box

The box described by the addition of the leading to the content area. For nonreplaced elements, the height of the inline box of an element will be equal to the value for line-height. For replaced elements, the height of the inline box of an element will be equal to the content area, as leading is not applied to replaced elements.

Line box

The shortest box that bounds the highest and lowest points of the inline boxes that are found in the line. In other words, the top edge of the line box will be placed along the top of the highest inline box top, and the bottom of the line box is placed along the bottom of the lowest inline box bottom. (See Figure 3.)

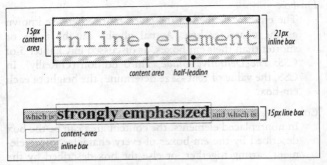

Figure 3. Inline layout details

Floating Rules

Floating allows an element to be placed to the left or right of its containing block (which is the nearest block-level ancestor element), with following content flowing around the element. A floated element is placed according to the following rules:

- The left (or right) outer edge of a floated element may not be to the left (or right) of the inner edge of its containing block.

- The left (or right) outer edge of a floated element must be to the right (or left) of the right (left) outer edge of a left-floating (or right-floating) element that occurs earlier in the document's source, unless the top of the later element is below the bottom of the former.

- The right outer edge of a left-floating element may not be to the right of the left outer edge of any right-floating element to its right. The left outer edge of a right-floating element may not be to the left of the right outer edge of any left-floating element to its left.

- A floating element's top may not be higher than the inner top of its containing block.

- A floating element's top may not be higher than the top of any earlier floating or block-level element.
- A floating element's top may not be higher than the top of any line box with content that precedes the floating element.
- A left (or right) floating element that has another floating element to its left (right) may not have its right outer edge to the right (left) of its containing block's right (left) edge.
- A floating element must be placed as high as possible.
- A left-floating element must be put as far to the left as possible, a right-floating element as far to the right as possible. A higher position is preferred to one that is further to the right or left.

Positioning Rules

When elements are positioned, a number of special rules come into play. These rules govern not only the containing block of the element but also how it is laid out within that element.

Types of Positioning

Static positioning

The element's box is generated as normal. Block-level elements generate a rectangular box that is part of the document's flow, and inline-level boxes generate one or more line boxes that flow within their parent element.

Relative positioning

The element's box is offset by some distance. Its containing block can be considered to be the area that the element would occupy if it were not positioned. The element retains the shape it would have had were it not positioned, and the space that the element would ordinarily have occupied is preserved.

Absolute positioning

The element's box is completely removed from the flow of the document and positioned with respect to its containing block, which may be another element in the document or the initial containing block (described in the next section). Whatever space the element might have occupied in the normal document flow is closed up, as though the element did not exist. The positioned element generates a block box, regardless of the type of box it would generate if it were in the normal flow.

Fixed positioning

The element's box behaves as though it were set to absolute, but its containing block is the viewport itself.

The Containing Block

The containing block of a positioned element is determined as follows:

1. The containing block of the *root element* (also called the *initial containing block*) is established by the user agent. In HTML, the root element is the html element, although some browsers may use body.

2. For nonroot elements, if an element's position value is relative or static, its containing block is formed by the content edge of the nearest block-level, table-, cell-, or inline-block ancestor box. (Despite this rule, relatively positioned elements are still simply offset, not positioned with respect to the containing block described here.)

3. For nonroot elements that have a position value of absolute, the containing block is set to the nearest ancestor (of any kind) that has a position value other than static. This happens as follows:

   a. If the ancestor is block-level, the containing block is that element's padding edge; in other words, it is the area that would be bounded by a border.

b. If the ancestor is inline-level, the containing block is set to the content edge of the ancestor. In left-to-right languages, the top and left of the containing block are the top and left content edges of the first box in the ancestor, and the bottom and right edges are the bottom and right content edges of the last box. In right-to-left languages, the right edge of the containing block corresponds to the right content edge of the first box, and the left is taken from the last box. The top and bottom are the same.

c. If there are no ancestors as described in 3a and 3b, then the absolutely positioned element's containing block is defined to be the initial containing block.

Layout of Absolutely Positioned Elements

In the following sections, these terms are used:

Shrink-to-fit
Similar to calculating the width of a table cell using the automatic table layout algorithm. In general, the user agent attempts to find the minimum element width that will contain the content and wrap to multiple lines only if wrapping cannot be avoided.

Static position
The place where an element's edge would have been placed if its position were static.

Horizontal layout of nonreplaced absolutely positioned elements

The equation that governs the layout of these elements is:

```
left + margin-left + border-left-width + padding-left
+ width + padding-right + border-right-width + margin-
right + right = width of containing block
```

The steps used to determine layout are:

1. If all of `left`, `width`, and `right` are `auto`, first reset any auto values for `margin-left` and `margin-right` to 0. Then, if `direction` is `ltr`, set `left` to the static position and apply the rule given in step 3c. Otherwise, set `right` to the static position and apply the rule given in step 3a.

2. If none of `left`, `width`, and `right` is `auto`, pick the rule that applies from the following list:

   a. If both `margin-left` and `margin-right` are set to `auto`, solve the equation under the additional constraint that the two margins get equal values.

   b. If only one of `margin-left` or `margin-right` is set to `auto`, solve the equation for that value.

   c. If the values are overconstrained (none is set to `auto`), ignore the value for `left` if `direction` is `rtl` (ignore `right` if `direction` is `ltr`) and solve for that value.

3. If some of `left`, `width`, and `right` are `auto`, but others are not, reset any auto values for `margin-left` and `margin-right` to 0. From the following list, pick the one rule that applies:

   a. If `left` and `width` are `auto` and `right` is not, then the width is shrink-to-fit. Solve the equation for `left`.

   b. If `left` and `right` are `auto` and `width` is not, then if `direction` is `ltr`, set `left` to the static position (otherwise, set `right` to the static position). Solve the equation for `left` (if `direction` is `rtl`) or `right` (if `direction` is `ltr`).

   c. If `width` and `right` are `auto` and `left` is not, then the width is shrink-to-fit. Solve the equation for `right`.

   d. If `left` is `auto` and `width` and `right` are not, solve the equation for `left`.

   e. If `width` is `auto` and `left` and `right` are not, solve the equation for `width`.

   f. If `right` is `auto` and `left` and `width` are not, solve the equation for `right`.

Vertical layout of nonreplaced absolutely positioned elements

The equation that governs the layout of these elements is:

```
top + margin-top + border-top-width + padding-top + height
+ padding-bottom + border-bottom-width + margin-bottom +
bottom = height of containing block
```

The steps used to determine layout are:

1. If all of top, height, and bottom are auto, set top to the static position and apply the rule given in step 3c.

2. If none of top, height, and bottom is auto, pick the one rule that applies from the following list:

   a. If both margin-top and margin-bottom are set to auto, solve the equation under the additional constraint that the two margins get equal values.

   b. If only one of margin-top or margin-bottom is set to auto, solve the equation for that value.

   c. If the values are overconstrained (none is set to auto), ignore the value for bottom and solve for that value.

3. If some of top, height, and bottom are auto, but others are not, pick the one rule that applies from the following list:

   a. If top and height are auto and bottom is not, then the height is based on the element's content (as it would be in the static flow). Reset any auto values for margin-top and margin-bottom to 0 and solve the equation for top.

   b. If top and bottom are auto and height is not, then set top to the static position. Reset any auto values for margin-top and margin-bottom to 0 and solve the equation for bottom.

   c. If height and bottom are auto and top is not, then the height is based on the element's content (as it would be in the static flow). Reset any auto values for margin-top and margin-bottom to 0 and solve the equation for bottom.

d. If top is auto and height and bottom are not, reset any auto values for margin-top and margin-bottom to 0 and solve the equation for top.

e. If height is auto and top and bottom are not, reset any auto values for margin-top and margin-bottom to 0 and solve the equation for height.

f. If bottom is auto and top and height are not, reset any auto values for margin-top and margin-bottom to 0 and solve the equation for bottom.

Horizontal layout of replaced absolutely positioned elements

The behaviors that go into placing and sizing replaced elements are most easily expressed as a series of rules to be taken one after the other. These rules state:

1. If width is set to auto, the computed value of width is determined by the intrinsic width of the element's content. Thus, the width of an image 50 pixels wide is computed to be 50px. If width is explicitly declared (that is, something such as 100px or 50%), then the width is set to that value.

2. If left has the value auto in a left-to-right language, replace auto with the static position. In right-to-left languages, replace an auto value for right with the static position.

3. If either left or right is still auto (in other words, it hasn't been replaced in a previous step), replace any auto value in margin-left or margin-right with 0.

4. If at this point both margin-left and margin-right are still defined to be auto, set them to be equal, thus centering the element in its containing block.

5. After all that, if there is only one auto value left, change it to equal the remainder of the equation.

Vertical layout of replaced absolutely positioned elements

The behaviors that go into placing and sizing replaced elements are most easily expressed as a series of rules to be taken one after the other. These state:

1. If `height` is set to auto, the computed value of `height` is determined by the intrinsic height of the element's content. Thus, the height of an image 50 pixels tall is computed to be 50px. If `height` is explicitly declared (that is, something such as 100px or 50%), then the height is set to that value.

2. If `top` has the value auto, replace the value with the replaced element's static position.

3. If `bottom` has a value of auto, replace any auto value on `margin-top` or `margin-bottom` with 0.

4. If at this point both `margin-top` and `margin-bottom` are still defined to be auto, set them to be equal, thus centering the element in its containing block.

5. After all that, if there is only one auto value left, change it to equal the remainder of the equation.

Table Layout

The layout of tables can get quite complicated, especially because CSS defines two different ways to calculate table and cell widths, as well as two ways to handle the borders of tables and elements internal to the table. Figure 4 illustrates the components of a table.

Table Arrangement Rules

In general, a table is laid out according to the following principles:

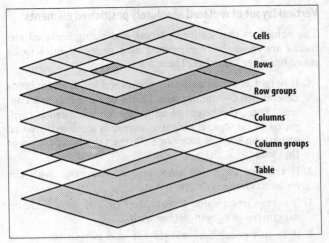

Figure 4. Table layout components

- Each row box encompasses a single row of grid cells. All of the row boxes in a table fill the table from top to bottom in the order they occur in the source document. Thus, the table contains as many grid rows as there are row elements.

- A row group's box encompasses the same grid cells as the row boxes that it contains.

- A column box encompasses one or more columns of grid cells. Column boxes are placed next to each other in the order they occur. The first column box is on the left for left-to-right languages and on the right for right-to-left languages.

- A column group's box encompasses the same grid cells as the column boxes that it contains.

- Although cells may span several rows or columns, CSS does not define how that happens. It is instead left to the document language to define spanning. Each spanned cell is a rectangular box one or more grid cells wide and high. The top row of this rectangle is in the row that is parent to the cell. The cell's rectangle must be as far to the left as possible in left-to-right languages, but it may not overlap any other cell box. It must also be to the right of all cells in the same row that are earlier in the source document in a left-to-right language. In right-to-left languages, a spanned cell must be as far to the right as possible without overlapping other cells and must be to the left of all cells in the same row that come after it in the document source.

- A cell's box cannot extend beyond the last row box of a table or row group. If the table structure causes this condition, the cell must be shortened until it fits within the table or row group that encloses it.

Fixed Table Layout

The fixed-layout model is fast because its layout doesn't depend on the contents of table cells; it's driven by the width values of the table, columns, and cells within the first row of the table. The fixed-layout model uses the following simple steps:

1. Any column element whose width property has a value other than auto sets the width for that column.

2. If a column has an auto width, but the cell in the first row of the table within that column has a width other than auto, then that cell sets the width for that column. If the cell spans multiple columns, then the width is divided equally among the columns.

3. Any columns that are still auto-sized are sized so that their widths are as equal as possible.

At that point, the width of the table is set to be either the value of width for the table or the sum of the column widths, whichever is greater. If the table turns out to be wider than the column widths, the difference is divided by the number of columns and added to each of them.

Automatic Table Layout

The automatic-layout model, although not as fast as the fixed-layout, is likely to be much more familiar to authors because it's substantially the same model that HTML tables have used for years. In most current user agents, use of this model will be triggered by a table with a width of auto, regardless of the value of table-layout—although this is not assured.

The details of the model can be expressed in the following steps:

1. For each cell in a column, calculate both the minimum and maximum cell width.

2. Determine the minimum width required to display the content. In determining the minimum content width, the content can flow to any number of lines, but it may not stick out of the cell's box. If the cell has a width value that is larger than the minimum possible width, then the minimum cell width is set to the value of width. If the cell's width value is auto, then the minimum cell width is set to the minimum content width.

3. For the maximum width, determine the width required to display the content without any line-breaking, other than that forced by explicit line-breaking (e.g., due to the <br> element). That value is the maximum cell width.

4. For each column, calculate both the minimum and maximum column width.

   a. The column's minimum width is determined by the largest minimum cell width of the cells within the column. If the column has been given an explicit width value that is larger than any of the minimum cell widths within the column, then the minimum column width is set to the value of width.

   b. For the maximum width, take the largest maximum cell width of the cells within the column. If the column has been given an explicit width value that is larger than any of the maximum cell widths within the column, then the maximum column width is set to the value of width. These two behaviors recreate the traditional HTML table behavior of forcibly expanding any column to be as wide as its widest cell.

5. In cases where a cell spans more than one column, the sum of the minimum column widths must be equal to the minimum cell width for the spanning cell. Similarly, the sum of the maximum column widths must equal the spanning cell's maximum width. User agents should divide any changes in column widths equally among the spanned columns.

In addition, the user agent must take into account that when a column width has a percentage value for its width, the percentage is calculated in relation to the width of the table—even though that width is not known yet. The user agent must hang on to the percentage value and use it in the next part of the algorithm. Once the user agent has determined how wide or narrow each column can be, it can calculate the width of the table. This happens as follows:

1. If the computed width of the table is not auto, then the computed table width is compared to the sum of all the column widths plus any borders and cell-spacing. (Columns with percentage widths are likely calculated at this time.) The larger of the two values is the final width of the table. If the table's computed width is larger than the sum of the column widths, borders, and cell-spacing, then all columns are increased in width by an equal amount so they fill the computed width of the table.

2. If the computed width of the table is auto, then the final width of the table is determined by summing up the column widths, borders, and cell-spacing. This means the table will be only as wide as needed to display its content, just as with traditional HTML tables. Any columns with percentage widths use that percentage as a constraint, but it is a constraint that a user agent does not have to satisfy.

Once the last step is completed, then (and only then) can the user agent actually lay out the table.

Collapsing Cell Borders

The collapsing cell model largely describes how HTML tables have always been laid out when they have no cell-spacing. The following rules govern this model:

- Table elements cannot have any padding, although they can have margins. Thus, there is never separation between the border around the outside of the table and its outermost cells.
- Borders can be applied to cells, rows, row groups, columns, and column groups. The table element itself can, as always, have a border.
- There is never any separation between cell borders. In fact, borders collapse into each other where they adjoin so that only one of the collapsing borders is actually drawn. This is somewhat akin to margin-collapsing, where the largest margin wins. When cell borders collapse, the "most interesting" border wins.
- Once they are collapsed, the borders between cells are centered on the hypothetical grid lines between the cells.

Collapsing borders

When two or more borders are adjacent, they collapse into each other, as shown in Figure 5. There are some strict rules governing which borders will win and which will not:

1. If one of the collapsing borders has a border-style of hidden, it takes precedence over all other collapsing borders: all borders at this location are hidden.

2. If one of the collapsing borders has a border-style of none, it takes the lowest priority. There will be no border drawn at this location only if all of the borders meeting at this location have a value of none. Note that none is the default value for border-style.

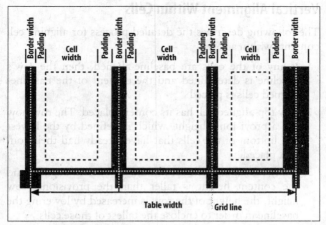

Figure 5. Collapsing cell borders model

3. If at least one of the collapsing borders has a value other than either none or hidden, then narrow borders lose out to wider ones. If two or more of the collapsing borders have the same width, then the border style is taken in the following order, from most preferred to least: double, solid, dashed, dotted, ridge, outset, groove, inset. Thus, if two borders with the same width collapse and one is dashed while the other is outset, the border at that location will be dashed.

4. If collapsing borders have the same style and width but differ in color, the color used is taken from an element in the following list, from most preferred to least: cell, row, row group, column, column group, table. Thus, if the borders of a cell and a column—identical in every way except color—collapse, then the cell's border color (and style and width) will be used. If the collapsing borders come from the same type of element—such as two row borders with the same style and width, but different colors—then the one furthest to the left and top wins in left-to-right languages; in right-to-left languages, the cell furthest to the right and top wins.

Vertical Alignment Within Cells

The following describes the detailed process for aligning cell contents within a row:

1. If any of the cells are baseline-aligned, then the row's baseline is determined and the content of the baseline-aligned cells is placed.

2. Any top-aligned cell has its content placed. The row now has a provisional height, which is defined by the lowest cell bottom of the cells that have already had their content placed.

3. If any remaining cells are middle- or bottom-aligned, and the content height is taller than the provisional row height, the height of the row is increased by lowering the baseline in order to enclose the tallest of those cells.

4. All remaining cells have their content placed. In any cell with contents shorter than the row height, the cell's padding is increased in order to match the height of the row.

Values

There are a variety of value types in CSS, most of which use units. Combining basic value types (such as numbers) with units (such as pixels) makes it possible to do any number of interesting things with CSS.

Keywords

Keywords are defined on a per-property basis and have a meaning specific only to a given property. For example, normal has totally unique meanings for the properties font-variant and letter-spacing. Keywords, as are property names, are not case-sensitive. A special case is the keyword inherit, which is allowed on all properties and always has the same meaning (get the associated property's value from the element's parent).

Color Values

#RRGGBB

This is a hex-pair notation familiar to authors using traditional HTML. In this format, the first pair of digits corresponds to the red level, the second pair to the green, and the third pair to the blue. Each pair is in hexadecimal notation in the range 00-FF. Thus, a "pure" blue is written #0000FF, a "pure" red is written #FF0000, and so on.

#RGB

This is a shorter form of the six-digit notation described above. In this format, each digit is replicated to arrive at an equivalent six-digit value; thus, #F8C becomes #FF88CC.

rgb (rrr.rr%,ggg.gg%,bbb.bb%)

This format allows the author to use RGB values in the range 0% to 100%, with decimal values allowed (e.g., 75.5%). The value for black is thus rgb (0%,0%,0%), whereas "pure" blue is rgb (0%,0%,100%).

rgb (rrr,ggg,bbb)

Similar to the previous value; the differences here are that the accepted range of values is 0-255 and only integers are permitted. Not coincidentally, this range is the decimal equivalent of 00-FF in hexadecimal. In this format, "pure" green is rgb (0,255,0), and white is represented as rgb (255,255,255).

<keyword>

One of 17 recognized keywords based largely on the original Windows VGA colors. These keywords are aqua, black, blue, fuchsia, gray, green, lime, maroon, navy, olive, orange, purple, red, silver, teal, white, and yellow. Browsers may recognize other keywords, such as the X11 color keywords that are documented in the W3C CSS3 Color Module specification.

Number Values

A number value is expressed as a positive or negative number (when permitted). Numbers can be either real or integers, and some properties or value types may restrict number values to integers. They may also restrict the range of acceptable values, as with color values that accept only integers in the range 0–255.

Percentage Values

A percentage value is expressed as a positive or negative number (when permitted), followed immediately by a percent sign (%). There should never be any space between the number and the percent sign. A percentage value will always be computed relative to something else. For example, declaring font-size: 120%; for an element sets its font size to 120% of the computed font-size of its parent element.

Length Values

A length value is expressed as a positive or negative number (when permitted), followed immediately by a two-letter abbreviation that represents the units to be used. There should never be any space between the number and the unit designator. Note that a value of 0 (zero) need not have a unit designator. Length units are divided into two types: *absolute units*, which are (in theory) always measured in the same way, and *relative units*, which are measured in relation to other things.

Absolute length units

Inches (in)
> As you might expect, the same inches found on typical U.S. rulers. The mapping from inches to a monitor or other display device is usually approximate at best

because many systems have no concept of the relation of their display areas to "real-world" measurements such as inches. Thus, inches should be used with extreme caution in screen design.

Centimeters (cm)

The centimeters found on rulers the world over. There are 2.54 cm to an inch, and 1 centimeter equals 0.394 inches. The same mapping warnings that applied to inches also apply to centimeters.

Millimeters (mm)

There are 10 millimeters to a centimeter, so you get 25.4 mm to an inch, and 1 millimeter equals 0.0394 inches. Bear in mind the previous warnings about mapping lengths to monitors.

Points (pt)

Points are standard typographical measures used by printers and typesetters for decades and by word-processing programs for many years. By modern definition, there are 72 points to an inch. Therefore, the capital letters of text set to 12 points should be one-sixth of an inch tall. For example, p {font-size: 18pt;} is equivalent to p {font-size: 0.25in;}, assuming proper mapping of lengths to the display environment (see comments above).

Picas (pc)

Another typographical term. A pica is equivalent to 12 points, which means there are 6 picas to an inch. The capital letters of text set to 1 pica should be one-sixth of an inch tall. For example, p {font-size: 1.5pc;} would set text to be the same size as the example declarations found in the definition of points. Keep in mind previous warnings.

Relative length units

em-height (em)

This refers to the em-height of a given font. In CSS, the em-height is equivalent to the height of the character box for a given font. Ems can be used to set relative sizes for fonts; for example, 1.2em is the same as saying 120%.

x-height (ex)

This refers to the x-height of the font. However, the vast majority of fonts do not include their x-height, so many browsers approximate it (poorly) by simply setting 1ex to be equal to 0.5em. The exception is IE5/Mac, which attempts to determine the actual x-height of a font by internally bitmapping a very large "x" and counting pixels!

Pixels (px)

A pixel is a small box on screen, but CSS defines pixels more abstractly. In CSS terms, a pixel is defined to be about the size required to yield 96 pixels per inch. Most user agents ignore this definition in favor of simply addressing the pixels on the monitor. Scaling factors are brought into play when printing, although this scale cannot be relied upon.

URIs

<uri>

Used to point to a file such as a graphic. CSS defines URIs as relative to a style sheet. URI stands for Uniform Resource Identifier, which is the new name for URLs. (Technically, URLs are a subset of URIs.) In CSS, which was first defined when URIs were still called URLs, this means that references to URIs will actually appear in the form url(<uri>). Fun!

Aural-Specific Values

The following values are used in conjunction with aural style properties in CSS2. These values were dropped from CSS2.1 due to a lack of support and are included here for the sake of completeness.

Angle values
> Used to define the position from which a given sound should seem to originate. There are three types of angles: degrees (deg), grads (grad), and radians (rad). For example, a right angle could be declared as 90deg, 100grad, or 1.57rad; in each case, the values are translated into degrees in the range 0 through 360. This is also true of negative values, which are allowed. The measure -90deg is the same as 270deg.

Time values
> Used to specify delays between speaking elements. Time values can be expressed as either milliseconds (ms) or seconds (s); thus, 100ms and 0.1s are equivalent. They cannot be negative, as CSS is supposed to avoid temporal paradoxes.

Frequency values
> Used to declare frequencies for the sounds that speaking browsers can produce. Frequency values can be expressed as hertz (Hz) or megahertz (mHz) and cannot be negative. The value labels are case-insensitive, so 10mHz and 10mhz are equivalent.

Selectors

Universal Selector

Pattern:

```
*
```

Description:

This selector matches any element name in the document's language. If a rule does not have an explicit selector, then the universal selector is inferred.

Examples:

```
* {color: red;}
div * p {color: blue;}
```

Supported by:

All CSS-aware browsers.

Type Selector

Pattern:

```
element1
```

Description:

This selector matches the name of an element in the document's language. Every instance of the element name is matched. (CSS1 referred to these as "element selectors.")

Examples:

```
body {background: #FFF;}
p {font-size: 1em;}
```

Supported by:

All CSS-aware browsers.

Descendant Selector

Pattern:

```
element1 element2
```

Description:

This allows the author to select an element based on its status as a descendant of another element. The matched element can be a child, grandchild, great-grandchild, etc., of the ancestor element. (CSS1 referred to these as "contextual selectors.")

Examples:

```
body h1 {font-size: 200%;}
table tr td div ul li {color: purple;}
```

Supported by:

All CSS-aware browsers.

Child Selector

Pattern:

```
element1 > element2
```

Description:

This type of selector is used to match an element based on its status as a child of another element. It is more restrictive than a descendant selector, as only a child will be matched.

Examples:

```
div > p {color: cyan;}
ul > li {font-weight: bold;}
```

Supported by:

Firefox, Internet Explorer 7+ only, Opera, Safari.

Adjacent Sibling Selector

Pattern:

element1 + element2

Description:

This allows the author to select an element that is the following adjacent sibling of another element. Any text between the two elements is ignored; only elements and their positions in the document tree are considered.

Examples:

```
table + p {margin-top: 2.5em;}
h1 + * {margin-top: 0;}
```

Supported by:

Firefox, Internet Explorer 7+ only, Opera, Safari.

Class Selector

Pattern:

element1.classname

element1.classname1.classname2

Description:

In languages that permit it, such as HTML, XHTML, SVG, and MathML, a class selector using "dot notation" can be used to select elements that have a class attribute containing a specific value or values. The name of the class value must immediately follow the dot. Multiple class values can be chained together, although there are support problems in Explorer previous to IE7. If no element name precedes the dot, then the selector matches all elements bearing that class value or values.

Examples:

```
p.urgent {color: red;}
a.external {font-style: italic;}
.example {background: olive;}
.note.caution {background: yellow;}
```

Supported by:

All CSS-aware browsers.

Note:

IE previous to IE7 does not support the chained selector syntax, though it does permit multiple words in class values in the markup.

ID Selector

Pattern:

element1#idname

Description:

In languages that permit it, such as HTML or XHTML, an ID selector using "hash notation" can be used to select elements that have an ID containing a specific value or values. The name of the ID value must immediately follow the octothorpe (#). If no element name precedes the octothorpe, then the selector matches all elements containing that ID value.

Examples:

```
h1#page-title {font-size: 250%;}
body#home {background: silver;}
#example {background: lime;}
```

Supported by:

All CSS-aware browsers.

Simple Attribute Selector

Pattern:

element1[attr]

Description:

This allows authors to select any element based on the presence of an attribute, regardless of the attribute's value.

Examples:

```
a[rel] {border-bottom: 3px double gray;}
p[class] {border: 1px dotted silver;}
```

Supported by:

Firefox, Internet Explorer 7+ only, Opera, Safari.

Exact Attribute Value Selector

Pattern:

element1[attr="value"]

Description:

This allows authors to select any element based on the precise and complete value of an attribute.

Examples:

```
a[rel="Start"] {font-weight: bold;}
p[class="urgent"] {color: red;}
```

Supported by:

Firefox, Internet Explorer 7+ only, Opera, Safari.

Partial Attribute Value Selector

Pattern:

element1[attr~="value"]

Description:

This allows authors to select any element based on a portion of the space-separated value of an attribute. Note that [class~="value"] is equivalent to .value (see above).

Examples:

```
a[rel|="friend"] {text-transform: uppercase;}
p[class|="warning"] {background: yellow;}
```

Supported by:

Firefox, Internet Explorer 7+ only, Opera, Safari.

Beginning Substring Attribute Value Selector

Pattern:

```
element1[attr^="substring"]
```

Description:

This allows authors to select any element based on a substring at the very beginning of an attribute's value.

Examples:

```
a[href^="/blog"] {text-transform: uppercase;}
p[class^="test-"] {background: yellow;}
```

Supported by:

Firefox, Internet Explorer 7+ only, Opera, Safari.

Ending Substring Attribute Value Selector

Pattern:

```
element1[attr$="substring"]
```

Description:

This allows authors to select any element based on a substring at the very end of an attribute's value.

Example:

```
a[href$=".pdf"] {font-style: italic;}
```

Supported by:

Firefox, Internet Explorer 7+ only, Opera, Safari.

Arbitrary Substring Attribute Value Selector

Pattern:

element1[attr*="substring"]

Description:

This allows authors to select any element based on a substring found anywhere within an attribute's value.

Examples:

```
a[href*="oreilly.com"] {font-weight: bold;}
div [class*="port"] {border: 1px solid red;}
```

Supported by:

Firefox, Internet Explorer 7+ only, Opera, Safari.

Language Attribute Selector

Pattern:

element1[lang|="lc"]

Description:

This allows authors to select any element with a lang attribute whose value is a hyphen-separated list of values, starting with the value provided in the selector.

Example:

```
html[lang|="tr"] {color: red;}
```

Supported by:

Firefox, Internet Explorer 7+ only, Opera, Safari.

Pseudo-Classes and Pseudo-Elements

:active

Type:
Pseudo-class.

Applies to:
An element that is being activated.

Description:
This applies to an element during the period in which it is being activated. The most common example is clicking on a hyperlink in an HTML document: while the mouse button is being held down, the link is active. There are other ways to activate elements, and other elements can in theory be activated, although CSS doesn't define them.

Examples:
```
a:active {color: red;}
*:active {background: blue;}
```

Supported by:
Firefox, Internet Explorer, Opera 6+, Safari.

:after

Type:
Pseudo-element.

Generates:
A pseudo-element containing generated content placed after the content in the element.

Description:

This allows the author to insert generated content at the end of an element's content. By default, the pseudo-element is inline, but it can be changed using the property display.

Examples:

```
a.external:after {content: " " url(/icons/globe.gif);}
p:after {content: " | ";}
```

Supported by:

Firefox, Opera, Safari.

:before

Type:

Pseudo-element.

Generates:

A pseudo-element containing generated content placed before the content in the element.

Description:

This allows the author to insert generated content at the beginning of an element's content. By default, the pseudo-element is inline, but that can be changed using the property display.

Examples:

```
a[href]:before {content: "[LINK] ";}
p:before {content: attr(class);}
a[rel|="met"]:after {content: " *";}
```

Supported by:

Firefox, Opera, Safari.

:first-child

Type:

Pseudo-class.

Applies to:

Any element that is the first child of another element.

Description:

With this pseudo-class, an element is matched only when it is the first child of another element. For example, `p:first-child` will select any p element that is the first child of some other element. It does *not*, as is commonly assumed, select whatever element is the first child of a paragraph; for that, an author would write `p > *:first-child`.

Examples:

```
body *:first-child {font-weight: bold;}
p:first-child {font-size: 125%;}
```

Supported by:

Firefox, Internet Explorer 7+, Opera, Safari.

:first-letter

Type:

Pseudo-element.

Generates:

A pseudo-element that contains the first letter of an element.

Description:

This is used to style the first letter of an element. Any leading punctuation should be styled along with the first letter. Some languages have letter combinations that should be treated as a single character, and a user agent may apply the first letter style to both. Prior to CSS2.1, `:first-letter` could be attached only to block-level elements. CSS2.1 expanded its scope to include block, list-item, table-call, table caption, and inline-block elements. There is a limited set of properties that can apply to a first letter.

Examples:

```
h1:first-letter {font-size: 166%;}
p:first-letter {text-decoration: underline;}
```

Supported by:

Firefox, Internet Explorer, Opera, Safari.

:first-line

Type:

Pseudo-element.

Generates:

A pseudo-element that contains the first formatted line of an element.

Description:

This is used to style the first line of text in an element, regardless of how many or how few words may appear in that line. :first-line can be attached only to block-level elements. There is a limited set of properties that can apply to a first line.

Example:

```
p.lead:first-line {font-weight: bold;}
```

Supported by:

Firefox, Internet Explorer, Opera, Safari.

:focus

Type:

Pseudo-class.

Applies to:

An element that has focus.

Description:

This applies to an element during the period in which it has focus. One example from HTML is an input box that has the text-input cursor within it such that when the user starts typing, text will be entered into that box. Other elements, such as hyperlinks, can also have focus; however, CSS does not define which elements may have focus.

Examples:

```
a:focus {outline: 1px dotted red;}
input:focus {background: yellow;}
```

Supported by:

Firefox, Internet Explorer, Opera, Safari.

Note:

:focus support in Explorer applies only to hyperlinks and does not extend to form controls.

:hover

Type:

Pseudo-class.

Applies to:

An element that is in a hovered state.

Description:

This applies to an element during the period in which it is being *hovered* (when the user is designating an element without activating it). The most common example of this is moving the mouse pointer inside the boundaries of a hyperlink in an HTML document. Other elements can in theory be hovered, although CSS doesn't define which ones.

Examples:

```
a[href]:hover {text-decoration: underline;}
p:hover {background: yellow;}
```

Supported by:

Firefox, Internet Explorer, Opera, Safari.

Note:

:hover support in Explorer applies only to hyperlinks in versions previous to IE7.

:lang

Type:

Pseudo-class.

Applies to:

Any element with associated language-encoding information.

Description:

This matches elements based on their human-language encoding. Such language information must be contained within or otherwise associated with the document; it cannot be assigned from CSS. The handling of :lang is the same as for |= attribute selectors. For example, in an HTML document, the language of an element is determined by its lang attribute. If the document does not have one, the language of an element is determined by the lang attribute of its nearest ancestor that does have one, and lacking that, by the Content-Language HTTP header response field (or the respective meta http-equiv) for the document.

Examples:

```
html:lang(en) {background: silver;}
*:lang(fr) {quotes: '&#171; ' ' &#187;';}
```

Supported by:

Firefox, Opera.

:link

Type:

Pseudo-class.

Applies to:

A hyperlink to another resource that has not been visited.

Description:

This applies to a link to a URI that has not been visited; that is, the URI to which the link points does not appear in the user agent's history. This state is mutually exclusive with the :visited state.

Examples:

```
a:link {color: blue;}
*:link {text-decoration: underline;}
```

Supported by:

Firefox, Internet Explorer, Opera, Safari.

:visited

Type:

Pseudo-class.

Applies to:

A hyperlink to another resource that has already been visited.

Description:

This applies to a link to a URI that has been visited; that is, the URI to which the link points appears in the user agent's history. This state is mutually exclusive with the :link state.

Examples:

```
a:visited {color: purple;}
*:visited {color: gray;}
```

Supported by:

Firefox, Internet Explorer, Opera, Safari.

Property Reference

Visual Media

background

Values:

[<background-color> || <background-image> || <background-repeat> || <background-attachment> || <background-position>] | inherit

Initial value:

Refer to individual properties.

Applies to:

All elements.

Inherited:

No.

Percentages:

Values are allowed for <background-position>.

Computed value:

See individual properties.

Description:

A shorthand way of expressing the various background properties using a single rule. Use of this property is encouraged over the other background properties because it is more widely supported and doesn't take as long to type. However, using it will set all of the allowed values (e.g., the repeat, position, and so on) to their defaults if the values are not explicitly declared. Thus, the following two rules will have the same appearance:

```
background: yellow;
background: yellow none top left repeat;
```

Furthermore, these defaults can override previous declarations made with more specific background properties. For example, given the following rules:

```
h1 {background-repeat: repeat-x;}
h1, h2 {background: yellow url(headback.gif);}
```

the repeat value for both h1 and h2 elements will be set to the default of repeat, overriding the previously declared value of repeat-x.

Examples:

```
body {background: white url(bg41.gif) fixed center repeat-x;}
p {background: url(http://www.pix.org/stone.png) #555;}
pre {background: yellow;}
```

Supported by:

Firefox, Internet Explorer, Opera, Safari.

Note:

There is limited support for background-attachment in Explorer previous to IE7.

background-attachment

Values:

scroll | fixed | inherit

Initial value:

scroll

Applies to:

All elements.

Inherited:

No.

Computed value:

As specified.

Description:

This property defines whether the background image scrolls along with the element when the document is scrolled. This property can be used to create "aligned" backgrounds; for more details, see Chapter 9 of *CSS: The Definitive Guide*, Third Edition (O'Reilly).

Examples:

```
body {background-attachment: scroll;}
div.fixbg {background-attachment: fixed;}
```

Supported by:

Firefox, Internet Explorer, Opera, Safari.

Note:

This property is supported only for the body element in Explorer previous to IE7.

background-color

Values:

<color> | transparent | inherit

Initial value:

transparent

Applies to:

All elements.

Inherited:

No.

Computed value:

As specified.

Description:

This property sets a solid color for the background of the element. This color fills the content, padding, and border areas of the element, extending to the outer edge of the element's border.

Borders that have transparent sections (such as dashed borders) will show the background color through the transparent sections.

Examples:

```
h4 {background-color: white;}
p {background-color: rgb(50%,50%,50%);}
pre {background-color: #FF9;}
```

Supported by:

Firefox, Internet Explorer, Opera, Safari.

---

background-image

Values:

<uri> | none | inherit

Initial value:

Applies to:

All elements.

Inherited:

No.

Computed value:

Absolute URI.

Description:

This property places an image in the background of the element. Depending on the value of background-repeat, the image may tile infinitely, along one axis, or not at all. The initial background image (the origin image) is placed according to the value of background-position.

Examples:

```
body {background-image: url(bg41.gif);}
h2 {background-image: url(http://www.pix.org/dots.png);}
```

Supported by:

Firefox, Internet Explorer, Opera, Safari.

background-position

Values:

[[<percentage> | <length> | left | center | right] [<percentage>
| <length> | top | center | bottom]?] | [[left | center | right] ||
[top | center | bottom]] | inherit

Initial value:

0% 0%

Applies to:

Block-level and replaced elements.

Inherited:

No.

Percentages:

Refer to the corresponding point on both the element and the origin image.

Computed value:

The absolute length offsets if <length> is specified; otherwise, percentage values.

Description:

This property sets the position of the background's origin image (as defined by background-image); this is the point from which any background repetition or tiling will occur. Percentage values define not only a point within the element, but also the same point in the origin image itself, thus allowing (for example) an image to be centered by declaring its position to be 50% 50%. For more details, see Chapter 9 of *CSS: The Definitive Guide*, Third Edition (O'Reilly).

When percentage or length values are used, the first is always the horizontal position, and the second the vertical. If only one value is given, it sets the horizontal position, while the missing value is assumed to be either center or 50%. Negative values are permitted and may place the origin image outside the element's content area without actually rendering it.

Examples:

```
body {background-position: top center;}
div#navbar {background-position: right;}
pre {background-position: 10px 50%;}
```

Supported by:

Firefox, Internet Explorer, Opera, Safari.

background-repeat

Values:

repeat | repeat-x | repeat-y | no-repeat | inherit

Initial value:

repeat

Applies to:

All elements.

Inherited:

No.

Computed value:

As specified.

Description:

This property defines the tiling pattern for the background image. Note that the axis-related repeat values actually cause repetition in both directions along the relevant axis. The repetition begins from the origin image, which is defined as the value of background-image and is placed according to the value of background-position.

Examples:

```
body {background-repeat: no-repeat;}
h2 {background-repeat: repeat-x;}
ul {background-repeat: repeat-y;}
```

Supported by:

Firefox, Internet Explorer, Opera, Safari.

border

Values:

[<border-width> || <border-style> || <border-color>] | inherit

Initial value:

Refer to individual properties.

Applies to:

All elements.

Inherited:

No.

Computed value:

As specified.

Description:

This is a shorthand property that defines the width, color, and style of an element's border. Note that while none of the values are actually required, omitting a border style will result in no border being applied because the default border style is none. Versions of IE/Win previous to IE5.5 do not apply borders to inline elements.

Examples:

```
h1 {border: 2px dashed olive;}
a:link {border: blue solid 1px;}
p.warning {border: double 5px red;}
```

Supported by:
Firefox, Internet Explorer, Opera, Safari.

border-bottom

Values:
[<border-width> || <border-style> || <border-color>] | inherit

Initial value:
Not defined for shorthand properties.

Applies to:
All elements.

Inherited:
No.

Computed value:
See individual properties (border-width, etc.).

Description:
This shorthand property defines the width, color, and style of the bottom border of an element. As with border, omission of a border style will result in no border appearing.

Examples:
```
ul {border-bottom: 0.5in groove green;}
a:active {border-bottom: purple 2px dashed;}
```

Supported by:
Firefox, Internet Explorer, Opera, Safari.

border-bottom-color

Values:
<color> | transparent | inherit

Initial value:

The value of color for the element.

Applies to:

All elements.

Inherited:

No.

Computed value:

If no value is specified, use the computed value of the property color for the same element; otherwise, as specified.

Description:

This property sets the color for the visible portions of the bottom border of an element. Only a solid color can be defined, and the border's style must be something other than none or hidden for any visible border to appear.

Examples:

```
ul {border-bottom-color: green;}
a:active {border-bottom-color: purple;}
```

Supported by:

Firefox, Internet Explorer, Opera, Safari.

border-bottom-style

Values:

none | hidden | dotted | dashed | solid | double | groove | ridge | inset | outset | inherit

Initial value:

Applies to:

All elements.

Inherited:

No.

Computed value:

As specified.

Description:

This defines the style for the bottom border of an element. The value must be something other than none for any border to appear.

Examples:

```
ul {border-bottom-style: groove;}
a:active {border-bottom-style: dashed;}
```

Supported by:

Firefox, Internet Explorer, Opera, Safari.

---

border-bottom-width

Values:

thin | medium | thick | <length> | inherit

Initial value:

medium

Applies to:

All elements.

Inherited:

No.

Computed value:

Absolute length; 0 if the style of the border is none or hidden.

Description:

This property sets the width for the bottom border of an element, which will take effect only if the border's style is something other than none. If the border style is none, then the border width is effectively reset to 0. Negative length values are not permitted.

Examples:

```
ul {border-bottom-width: 0.5in;}
a:active {border-bottom-width: 2px;}
```

Supported by:

Firefox, Internet Explorer, Opera, Safari.

---

border-color

Values:

[<color> | transparent]{1,4} | inherit

Initial value:

Not defined for shorthand properties.

Applies to:

All elements.

Inherited:

No.

Computed value:

See individual properties (border-top-color, etc.).

Description:

This shorthand property sets the color for the visible portions of the overall border of an element or sets a different color for each of the four sides. Remember that a border's style must be something other than none or hidden for any visible border to appear.

Examples:

```
h1 {border-color: purple;}
a:visited {border-color: maroon;}
```

Supported by:

Firefox, Internet Explorer, Opera, Safari.

border-left

Values:

[<border-width> || <border-style> || <border-color>] | inherit

Initial value:

Not defined for shorthand properties.

Applies to:

All elements.

Inherited:

No.

Computed value:

See individual properties (border-width, etc.).

Description:

This shorthand property defines the width, color, and style of the left border of an element. As with border, omission of a border style will result in no border appearing.

Examples:

```
p {border-left: 3em solid gray;}
pre {border-left: double black 4px;}
```

Supported by:

Firefox, Internet Explorer, Opera, Safari.

border-left-color

Values:

<color> | transparent | inherit

Initial value:

The value of color for the element.

Applies to:

All elements.

Inherited:

No.

Computed value:

If no value is specified, use the computed value of the property color for the same element; otherwise, as specified.

Description:

This property sets the color for the visible portions of the left border of an element. Only a solid color can be defined, and the border's style must be something other than none or hidden for any visible border to appear.

Examples:

```
p {border-left-color: gray;}
pre {border-left-color: black;}
```

Supported by:

Firefox, Internet Explorer, Opera, Safari.

border-left-style

Values:

none | hidden | dotted | dashed | solid | double | groove | ridge | inset | outset | inherit

Initial value:

Applies to:

All elements.

Inherited:

No.

Computed value:

As specified.

Description:

This defines the style for the left border of an element. The value must be something other than none for any border to appear.

Examples:

```
p {border-left-style: solid;}
pre {border-left-style: double;}
```

Supported by:

Firefox, Internet Explorer, Opera, Safari.

border-left-width

Values:

thin | medium | thick | <length> | inherit

Initial value:

medium

Applies to:

All elements.

Inherited:

No.

Computed value:

Absolute length; 0 if the style of the border is none or hidden.

Description:

This sets the width for the left border of an element, which will take effect only if the border's style is something other than none. If the border style is none, then the border width is effectively reset to 0. Negative length values are not permitted.

Examples:

```
p {border-left-width: 3em;}
pre {border-left-width: 4px;}
```

Supported by:
Firefox, Internet Explorer, Opera, Safari.

---

border-right

Values:
[<border-width> || <border-style> || <border-color>] | inherit

Initial value:
Not defined for shorthand properties.

Applies to:
All elements.

Inherited:
No.

Computed value:
See individual properties (border-width, etc.).

Description:
This shorthand property defines the width, color, and style of the right border of an element. As with border, omission of a border style will result in no border appearing.

Examples:

```
img {border-right: 30px dotted blue;}
h3 {border-right: cyan 1em inset;}
```

Supported by:
Firefox, Internet Explorer, Opera, Safari.

border-right-color

Values:

<color> | transparent | inherit

Initial value:

The value of color for the element.

Applies to:

All elements.

Inherited:

No.

Computed value:

If no value is specified, use the computed value of the property color for the same element; otherwise, as specified.

Description:

This property sets the color for the visible portions of the right border of an element. Only a solid color can be defined, and the border's style must be something other than none or hidden for any visible border to appear.

Examples:

```
img {border-right-color: blue;}
h3 {border-right-color: cyan;}
```

Supported by:

Firefox, Internet Explorer, Opera, Safari.

border-right-style

Values:

none | hidden | dotted | dashed | solid | double | groove | ridge | inset | outset | inherit

Initial value:

Applies to:

All elements.

Inherited:

No.

Computed value:

As specified.

Description:

This defines the style for the right border of an element. The value must be something other than none for any border to appear.

Examples:

```
img {border-right-style: dotted;}
h3 {border-right-style: inset;}
```

Supported by:

Firefox, Internet Explorer, Opera, Safari.

border-right-width

Values:

thin | medium | thick | <length> | inherit

Initial value:

medium

Applies to:

All elements.

Inherited:

No.

Computed value:

Absolute length; 0 if the style of the border is none or hidden.

Description:

This sets the width for the right border of an element, which will take effect only if the border's style is something other than none. If the border style is none, then the border width is effectively reset to 0. Negative length values are not permitted.

Examples:

```
img {border-right-width: 30px;}
h3 {border-right-width: 1em;}
```

Supported by:

Firefox, Internet Explorer, Opera, Safari.

---

border-style

Values:

[none | hidden | dotted | dashed | solid | double | groove | ridge | inset | outset]{1,4} | inherit

Initial value:

Not defined for shorthand properties.

Applies to:

All elements.

Inherited:

No.

Computed value:

See individual properties (border-top-style, etc.).

Description:

This shorthand property can be used to set the styles for the overall border of an element or for each side individually. The value of any border must be something other than none for the border to appear.

Note that setting border-style to none (its default value) will result in no border at all. In such a case, any value of border-width will be ignored and the width of the border will be set to 0. Any unrecognized value from the list of values should be reinterpreted as solid.

Examples:

```
h1 {border-style: solid;}
img {border-style: inset;}
```

Supported by:

Firefox, Internet Explorer, Opera, Safari.

border-top

Values:

[<border-width> || <border-style> || <border-color>] | inherit

Initial value:

Not defined for shorthand properties.

Applies to:

All elements.

Inherited:

No.

Computed value:

See individual properties (border-width, etc.).

Description:

This shorthand property defines the width, color, and style of the top border of an element. As with border, omission of a border style will result in no border appearing.

Examples:

```
ul {border-top: 0.5in solid black;}
h1 {border-top: dashed 1px gray;}
```

Supported by:

Firefox, Internet Explorer, Opera, Safari.

---

border-top-color

Values:

<color> | transparent | inherit

Initial value:

The value of color for the element.

Applies to:

All elements.

Inherited:

No.

Computed value:

If no value is specified, use the computed value of the property color for the same element; otherwise, as specified.

Description:

This property sets the color for the visible portions of the top border of an element. Only a solid color can be defined, and the border's style must be something other than none or hidden for any visible border to appear.

Examples:

```
ul {border-top-color: black;}
h1 {border-top-color: gray;}
```

Supported by:

Firefox, Internet Explorer, Opera, Safari.

border-top-style

Values:

none | hidden | dotted | dashed | solid | double | groove | ridge | inset | outset | inherit

Initial value:

Applies to:

All elements.

Inherited:

No.

Computed value:

As specified.

Description:

This defines the style for the top border of an element. The value must be something other than none for any border to appear.

Examples:

```
ul {border-top-style: solid;}
h1 {border-top-style: dashed;}
```

Supported by:

Firefox, Internet Explorer, Opera, Safari.

border-top-width

Values:

thin | medium | thick | <length> | inherit

Initial value:

Applies to:

All elements.

Inherited:

No.

Computed value:

Absolute length; 0 if the style of the border is none or hidden.

Description:

This sets the width for the top border of an element, which will take effect only if the border's style is something other than none. If the style is none, then the width is effectively reset to 0. Negative length values are not permitted.

Examples:

```
ul {border-top-width: 0.5in;}
h1 {border-top-width: 1px;}
```

Supported by:

Firefox, Internet Explorer, Opera, Safari.

border-width

Values:

[thin | medium | thick | <length>]{1,4} | inherit

Initial value:

Not defined for shorthand properties.

Applies to:

All elements.

Inherited:

No.

Computed value:

See individual properties (border-top-style, etc.).

Description:

This shorthand property can be used to set the width for the overall border of an element or for each side individually. The width will take effect for a given border only if the border's style is something other than none. If the border style is none, then the border width is effectively reset to 0. Negative length values are not permitted.

Examples:

```
h1 {border-width: 2ex;}
img {border-width: 5px;}
```

Supported by:

Firefox, Internet Explorer, Opera, Safari.

bottom

Values:

<length> | <percentage> | auto | inherit

Initial value:

auto

Applies to:

Positioned elements (that is, elements for which the value of position is something other than static).

Inherited:

No.

Percentages:

Refer to the height of the containing block.

Computed value:

For relatively positioned elements, see Note; for static elements, auto; for length values, the corresponding absolute length; for percentage values, the specified value; otherwise, auto.

Note:

For relatively positioned elements, if both bottom and top are auto, their computed values are both 0; if one of them is auto, it becomes the negative of the other; if neither is auto, bottom will become the negative of the value of top.

Description:

This property defines the offset between the bottom outer margin edge of a positioned element and the bottom edge of its containing block.

Examples:

```
div#footer {position: fixed; bottom: 0;}
sup {position: relative; bottom: 0.5em; vertical-align:
baseline;}
```

Supported by:

Firefox, Internet Explorer, Opera, Safari.

---

clear

Values:

left | right | both | none

Initial value:

Applies to:

Block-level elements.

Inherited:

No.

Computed value:

As specified.

Description:

This defines the sides of an element on which no floating elements may appear. In CSS1 and CSS2, this is accomplished by automatically increasing the top margin of the cleared element. In CSS2.1, clearance space is added above the element's top margin, but the margin itself is not altered. In either case, the end result is that the element's top outer border edge is just below the bottom outer margin edge of a floated element on the declared side.

Examples:

```
h1 {clear: both;}
h3 {clear: right;}
```

Supported by:

Firefox, Internet Explorer, Opera, Safari.

---

clip

Values:

rect(*top*, *right*, *bottom*, *left*) | auto | inherit

Initial value:

auto

Applies to:

Absolutely positioned elements (in CSS2, clip applied to block-level and replaced elements).

Inherited:

No.

Computed value:

For a rectangle, a set of four computed lengths representing the edges of the clipping rectangle; otherwise, as specified.

Description:

This is used to define a clipping rectangle inside of which the content of an absolutely positioned element is visible. Content outside the clipping area is treated according to the value of overflow. The clipping area can be smaller or larger than the content area of the element. In current browsers, the clipping area is defined by using the rect( ) value to define the offsets of the top, right, bottom, and left edges of the clipping areas with respect to the top left corner of the element. Thus, the value rect (5px, 10px, 40px, 5px) would place the top edge of the clipping area 5px down from the top edge of the element, the right edge of the clipping area 10px over from the left edge of the element, the bottom edge of the clipping area 40px down from the top edge of the element, and the left edge of the clipping area 5px over from the left edge of the element. Note that this behavior flatly contradicts CSS2.1, which defines the four values to define offsets from the top, right, bottom, and left sides of the element.

Examples:

```
div.sidebar {overflow: scroll; clip: 0 0 5em 10em;}
img.tiny {overflow: hidden; clip: 5px 5px 20px 20px;}
```

Supported by:

None as defined.

Firefox, Internet Explorer, Opera, Safari as described.

color

Values:

<color> | inherit

Initial value:

User agent-specific.

Applies to:

All elements.

Inherited:

Yes.

Computed value:

As specified.

Description:

This property sets the foreground color of an element, which in HTML rendering means the text of an element; raster images are not affected by color. This is also the color applied to any borders of the element, unless overridden by border-color or one of the other border color properties (border-top-color, etc.).

Examples:

```
strong {color: rgb (255,128,128);}
h3 {color: navy;}
p.warning {color: #ff0000;}
pre.pastoral {color: #0f0;}
```

Supported by:

Firefox, Internet Explorer, Opera, Safari.

---

content

Values:

normal | [<string> | <uri> | <counter> | attr(<identifier>)| open-quote | close-quote | no-open-quote | no-close-quote]+ | inherit

Initial value:

normal

Applies to:

:before and :after pseudo-elements.

Inherited:

No.

Computed value:

For <uri> values, an absolute URI; for attribute references, the resulting string; otherwise, as specified.

Description:

This is the property used to define the generated content placed before or after an element. By default, this is likely to be inline content, but the type of box the content creates can be controlled using the property display.

Examples:

```
p:before {content: "Paragraph...";}
img:after {content: attr(src);}
a[href]:after {content: "(" attr(href) ")"; font-size:
smaller;}
```

Supported by:

Firefox, Opera, Safari.

---

counter-increment

Values:

[<identifier> <integer>?]+ | none | inherit

Initial value:

User agent-dependent.

Applies to:

All elements.

Inherited:

No.

Computed value:

As specified.

Description:

With this property, counters can be incremented (or decremented) by any value, positive or negative. If no <integer> is supplied, it defaults to 1.

Examples:

```
h1 {counter-increment: section;}
*.backward li {counter-increment: counter -1;}
```

Supported by:

Opera.

---

counter-reset

Values:

[<identifier> <integer>?]+ | none | inherit

Initial value:

User agent-dependent.

Applies to:

All elements.

Inherited:

No.

Computed value:

As specified.

Description:

With this property, counters can be reset (or set for the first time) to any value, positive or negative. If no <integer> is supplied, it defaults to 0.

Examples:

```
h1 {counter-reset: section;}
h2 {counter-reset: subsec 1;}
```

Supported by:

None.

---

cursor

Values:

[[<uri>,]* [auto | default | pointer | crosshair | move | e-resize |
ne-resize | nw-resize | n-resize | se-resize | sw-resize | s-resize
| w-resize| text | wait | help | progress]] | inherit

Initial value:

auto

Applies to:

All elements.

Inherited:

Yes.

Computed value:

For <uri> values, an absolute URI; otherwise, as specified.

Description:

This defines the cursor shape to be used when a mouse pointer is
placed within the boundary of an element (although CSS2.1 does
not define which edge creates the boundary). Authors are
cautioned to remember that users are typically very aware of
cursor changes and can be easily confused by changes that seem
counterintuitive. For example, making any noninteractive element
switch the cursor state to pointer is quite likely to cause user
frustration.

<uri> values are supported only by IE6+/Win as of this writing.

Examples:

    a.moreinfo {cursor: help;}
    a[href].external {cursor: url(globe.ani);}

Supported by:

Firefox, Internet Explorer, Opera, Safari.

Note:

<uri> values are supported only by Explorer 6 and later.

direction

Values:

ltr | rtl | inherit

Initial value:

ltr

Applies to:

All elements.

Inherited:

Yes.

Computed value:

As specified.

Description:

This property specifies the base writing direction of blocks and the direction of embeddings and overrides for the unicode bidirectional algorithm. User agents that do not support bidirectional text are permitted to ignore this property.

Examples:

```
*:lang(en) {direction: ltr;}
*:lang(ar) {direction: rtl;}
```

Supported by:

Firefox, Internet Explorer, Opera, Safari.

display

Values:

none | inline | block | inline-block | list-item | run-in | table | inline-table | table-row-group | table-header-group | table-footer-group | table-row | table-column-group | table-column | table-cell | table-caption | inherit

Initial value:

inline

Applies to:

All elements.

Inherited:

No.

Computed value:

Varies for floated, positioned, and root elements (see CSS2.1, section 9.7); otherwise, as specified.

Note:

The values compact and marker appeared in CSS2 but were dropped from CSS2.1 due to a lack of widespread support.

Description:

This is used to define the kind of display box an element generates during layout. Gratuitous use of display with a document type such as HTML can be tricky, as it upsets the display hierarchy already defined in HTML, but it can also be very useful. In the case of XML, which has no such built-in hierarchy, display is indispensable.

Examples:

```
h1 {display: block;}
li {display: list-item;}
img {display: inline;}
.hide {display: none;}
tr {display: table-row;}
```

Supported by:

Firefox, Internet Explorer, Opera, Safari.

Note:

The table-related values are not supported by Internet Explorer.

---

float

Values:

left | right | none | inherit

Initial value:

Applies to:

All elements.

Inherited:

No.

Computed value:

As specified.

Description:

float defines the direction in which an element is floated. This has traditionally been applied to images in order to let text flow around them, but in CSS, any element may be floated. A floated element will generate a block-level box no matter what kind of element it may be. Floated nonreplaced elements should be given an explicit width, as they otherwise tend to become as narrow as possible. Basic floating is generally supported by all browsers, especially on images, but the nature of floats can lead to unexpected results when they are used as a page layout mechanism. Use float cautiously, and thoroughly test any pages employing it.

Examples:

```
img.figure {float: left;}
p.sidebar {float: right; width: 15em;}
```

Supported by:

Firefox, Internet Explorer, Opera, Safari.

---

font

Values:

[[<font-style> || <font-variant> || <font-weight>]? <font-size>
[/ <line-height>]? <font-family>] | caption | icon | menu |
message-box | small-caption | status-bar | inherit

Initial value:

Refer to individual properties.

Applies to:

All elements.

Inherited:

Yes.

Percentages:

Calculated with respect to the parent element for <font-size> and
with respect to the element's <font-size> for <line-height>.

Computed value:

See individual properties (font-style, etc.).

Description:

This is a shorthand property used to set two or more aspects of an
element's font at once. It can also be used to set the element's font to
match an aspect of the user's computing environment using
keywords such as icon. If keywords are not used, the minimum font
value must include the font size and family in that order.

Examples:

```
p {font: small-caps italic bold small/1.25em
Helvetica,sans-serif;}
p.example {font: 14px Arial;} /* technically correct,
although
```

```
    generic font-families are encouraged for fallback
    purposes */
.figure span {font: icon;}
```

Supported by:

Firefox, Internet Explorer, Opera, Safari.

---

font-family

Values:

[[<family-name> | <generic-family>],]* [<family-name> | <generic-family>] | inherit

Initial value:

User agent-specific.

Applies to:

All elements.

Inherited:

Yes.

Computed value:

As specified.

Description:

This defines a font family to be used in the display of an element's text. Note that use of a specific font family (e.g., Geneva) is wholly dependent on that family being available on a user's machine; no font downloading is implied by this property. Therefore, using generic family names as a fallback is strongly encouraged. Font names that contain spaces or nonalphabetic characters should be quoted to minimize potential confusion.

Examples:

```
p {font-family: Helvetica, Arial, sans-serif;}
li {font-family: Times, TimesNR, "New Century Schoolbook",
serif;}
pre {font-family: Courier, "Courier New", "Andale Mono",
Monaco, monospace;}
```

Supported by:

Firefox, Internet Explorer, Opera, Safari.

font-size

Values:

xx-small | x-small | small | medium | large | x-large | xx-large | smaller | larger | <length> | <percentage> | inherit

Initial value:

medium

Applies to:

All elements.

Inherited:

Yes.

Percentages:

Calculated with respect to the parent element's font size.

Computed value:

An absolute length.

Description:

This property sets the size of the font. The size can be defined as an absolute size, a relative size, a length value, or a percentage value. Negative length and percentage values are not permitted.

The dangers of font-size assignment are many and varied, and points are particularly discouraged in web design, as there is no certain relationship between points and the pixels on a monitor. It's a matter of historical interest that due to early misunderstandings, setting the font-size to medium led to different results in early versions of Internet Explorer and Navigator 4.x. Some of these problems are covered in Chapter 5 of *CSS: The Definitive Guide*, Third Edition (O'Reilly); for further discussion, refer to *http://style.cleverchimp.com/*.

For best results, authors are encouraged to use either percentages or em units for font sizing. As a last resort, pixel sizes can be used, but this approach has serious accessibility penalties because it prevents users from resizing text in IE/Win, even when it is too small to read comfortably. Most other browsers allow users to resize text regardless of how it has been sized.

Examples:

```
h2 {font-size: 200%;}
code {font-size: 0.9em;}
p.caption {font-size: 9px;}
```

Supported by:

Firefox, Internet Explorer, Opera, Safari.

font-style

Values:

italic | oblique | normal | inherit

Initial value:

normal

Applies to:

All elements.

Inherited:

Yes.

Computed value:

As specified.

Description:

This sets the font to use an italic, oblique, or normal font face. Italic text is generally defined as a separate face within the font family. It is theoretically possible for a user agent to compute a slanted font face from the normal face. However, the reality is that user agents rarely recognize the difference between italic and oblique text and almost always render both in exactly the same way.

Examples:
```
em {font-style: oblique;}
i {font-style: italic;}
```

Supported by:

Firefox, Internet Explorer, Opera, Safari.

font-variant

Values:

small-caps | normal | inherit

Initial value:

normal

Applies to:

All elements.

Inherited:

Yes.

Computed value:

As specified.

Description:

This property is basically used to define small-caps text. It is theoretically possible for a user agent to compute a small-caps font face from the normal face.

Examples:
```
h3 {font-variant: small-caps;}
p {font-variant: normal;}
```

Supported by:

Firefox, Internet Explorer, Opera, Safari.

font-weight

Values:

normal | bold | bolder | lighter | 100 | 200 | 300 | 400 | 500| 600 |
700 | 800 | 900 | inherit

Initial value:

normal

Applies to:

All elements.

Inherited:

Yes.

Computed value:

One of the numeric values (100, etc.) or one of the numeric values
plus one of the relative values (bolder or lighter).

Description:

This property sets the font weight used in rendering an element's
text. The numeric value 400 is equivalent to the keyword normal,
and 700 is equivalent to bold. Each numeric value must be at least
as light as the next lowest number and at least as heavy as the next
highest number. Thus, if a font has only two weights—normal
and bold—then the numbers 100 through 500 will be normal, and
600 through 900 will be bold.

Examples:

```
b {font-weight: 700;}
strong {font-weight: bold;}
.delicate {font-weight: lighter;}
```

Supported by:

Firefox, Internet Explorer, Opera, Safari.

Note:

There is minimal support for the numeric keywords (100-900).

height

Values:
<length> | <percentage> | auto | inherit

Initial value:
auto

Applies to:
Block-level and replaced elements.

Inherited:
No.

Percentages:
Calculated with respect to the height of the containing block.

Computed value:
For auto and percentage values, as specified; otherwise, an absolute length, unless the property does not apply to the element (then auto).

Description:
This defines the height of an element's content area, outside of which padding, borders, and margins are added. This property is ignored for inline nonreplaced elements. Negative length and percentage values are not permitted.

Examples:
```
img.icon {height: 50px;}
h1 {height: 1.75em;}
```

Supported by:
Firefox, Internet Explorer, Opera, Safari.

Note:
In IE6 and earlier, height is treated as a minimum height, not a fixed height.

left

Values:
<length> | <percentage> | auto | inherit

Initial value:
auto

Applies to:
Positioned elements (that is, elements for which the value of position is something other than static).

Inherited:
No.

Percentages:
Refer to the width of the containing block.

Computed value:
For relatively positioned elements, see Note; for static elements, auto; for length values, the corresponding absolute length; for percentage values, the specified value; otherwise, auto.

Note:
For relatively positioned elements, the computed value of left always equals -right.

Description:
This property defines the offset between the left outer margin edge of a positioned element and the left edge of its containing block.

Examples:
```
div#footer {position: fixed; left: 0;}
*.hanger {position: relative; left: -25px;}
```

Supported by:
Firefox, Internet Explorer, Opera, Safari.

letter-spacing

Values:

<length> | normal | inherit

Initial value:

normal

Applies to:

All elements.

Inherited:

Yes.

Computed value:

For length values, the absolute length; otherwise, normal.

Description:

This defines the amount of whitespace to be inserted between the character boxes of text. Because character glyphs are typically narrower than their character boxes, length values create a modifier to the usual spacing between letters. Thus, normal is synonymous with 0. Negative length values are permitted and will cause letters to bunch closer together.

Examples:

```
p.spacious {letter-spacing: 6px;}
em {letter-spacing: 0.2em;}
p.cramped {letter-spacing: -0.5em;}
```

Supported by:

Firefox, Internet Explorer, Opera, Safari.

line-height

Values:

<length> | <percentage> | <number> | normal | inherit

Initial value:

normal

Applies to:

All elements (but see text regarding replaced and block-level elements).

Inherited:

Yes.

Percentages:

Relative to the font size of the element.

Computed value:

For length and percentage values, the absolute value; otherwise, as specified.

Description:

This property influences the layout of line boxes. When applied to a block-level element, it defines the minimum (but not the maximum) distance between baselines within that element. The difference between the computed values of line-height and font-size (called "leading" in CSS) is split in half and added to the top and bottom of each piece of content in a line of text. The shortest box that can enclose all those pieces of content is the line box. A raw number value assigns a scaling factor, which is inherited instead of a computed value. Negative values are not permitted.

Examples:

```
p {line-height: 1.5em;}
h2 {line-height: 200%;}
ul {line-height: 1.2;}
pre {line-height: 0.75em;}
```

Supported by:

Firefox, Internet Explorer, Opera, Safari.

list-style

Values:

[<list-style-type> || <list-style-image> || <list-style-position>] | inherit

Initial value:

Refer to individual properties.

Applies to:

Elements whose display value is list-item.

Inherited:

Yes.

Computed value:

See individual properties.

Description:

This is a shorthand property that condenses all the other list-style properties. Because it applies to any element that has a display of list-item, it will apply only to li elements in ordinary HTML and XHTML, although it can be applied to any element and inherited by list-item elements.

Examples:

```
ul {list-style: square url(bullet3.gif) outer;} /* values
are inherited by 'li'
elements */
ol {list-style: upper-roman;}
```

Supported by:

Firefox, Internet Explorer, Opera, Safari.

list-style-image

Values:

<uri> | none | inherit

Initial value:

Applies to:

Elements whose display value is list-item.

Inherited:

Yes.

Computed value:

For <uri> values, the absolute URI; otherwise, none.

Description:

This specifies an image to be used as the marker on an ordered or unordered list item. The placement of the image with respect to the content of the list item can be broadly controlled using list-style-position.

Examples:

```
ul {list-style-image: url(bullet3.gif);}
ul li {list-style-image: url(http://example.org/pix/
checkmark.png);}
```

Supported by:

Firefox, Internet Explorer, Opera, Safari.

list-style-position

Values:

inside | outside | inherit

Initial value:

outside

Applies to:

Elements whose display value is list-item.

Inherited:

Yes.

Computed value:

As specified.

Description:

This property is used to declare the position of the list marker with respect to the content of the list item. Outside markers are placed some distance from the border edge of the list item, but the distance is not defined in CSS. Inside markers are treated as though they were inline elements inserted at the beginning of the list item's content.

Examples:

```
li {list-style-position: outside;}
ol li {list-style-position: inside;}
```

Supported by:

Firefox, Internet Explorer, Opera, Safari.

---

list-style-type

CSS2.1 values:

disc | circle | square | decimal | decimal-leading-zero | upper-alpha | lower-alpha | upper-latin | lower-latin | upper-roman | lower-roman | lower-greek | georgian | armenian | none | inherit

CSS2 values:

disc | circle | square | decimal | decimal-leading-zero | upper-alpha | lower-alpha | upper-latin | lower-latin | upper-roman | lower-roman | lower-greek | hebrew | armenian | georgian | cjk-ideographic | hiragana | katakana | hiragana-iroha | none | inherit

Initial value:

disc

Applies to:

Elements whose display value is list-item.

Inherited:

Yes.

Computed value:

As specified.

Description:

This is used to declare the type of marker system to be used in the presentation of a list. There is no defined behavior for what happens when a list using an alphabetic ordering exceeds the letters in the list. For example, once an upper-latin list reaches "Z", the specification does not say what the next bullet should be. (Two possible answers are "AA" and "ZA".) This is the case regardless of the alphabet in use. Thus, there is no guarantee that different user agents will act consistently.

Examples:

```
ul {list-style-type: square;}
ol {list-style-type: lower-roman;}
```

Supported by:

Firefox, Internet Explorer, Opera, Safari.

Note:

As of this writing, the only CSS2.1 values with widespread support are disc, circle, square, decimal, upper-alpha, lower-alpha, upper-latin, upper-roman, and lower-roman.

---

margin

Values:

[<length> | <percentage> | auto]{1,4} | inherit

Initial value:

Not defined.

Applies to:

All elements.

Inherited:

No.

Percentages:

Refer to the width of the containing block.

Computed value:

See individual properties.

Description:

This shorthand property sets the width of the overall margin for an element or sets the widths of each individual side margin. Vertically adjacent margins of block-level elements are collapsed, whereas inline elements effectively do not take top and bottom margins. The left and right margins of inline elements do not collapse, nor do margins on floated elements. Negative margin values are permitted, but caution is warranted because negative values can cause elements to overwrite other parts of a page or to appear to be wider than their parent elements.

Examples:

```
h1 {margin: 2ex;}
p {margin: auto;}
img {margin: 10px;}
```

Supported by:

Firefox, Internet Explorer, Opera, Safari.

margin-bottom

Values:

<length> | <percentage> | auto | inherit

Initial value:

0

Applies to:

All elements.

Inherited:

No.

Percentages:

Refer to the width of the containing block.

Computed value:

For percentages, as specified; for length values, the absolute length.

Description:

This sets the width of the bottom margin for an element. Negative values are permitted, but caution is warranted.

Examples:

```
ul {margin-bottom: 0.5in;}
h1 {margin-bottom: 2%;}
```

Supported by:

Firefox, Internet Explorer, Opera, Safari.

---

margin-left

Values:

<length> | <percentage> | auto | inherit

Initial value:

0

Applies to:

All elements.

Inherited:

No.

Percentages:

Refer to the width of the containing block.

Computed value:

For percentages, as specified; for length values, the absolute length.

Description:

This sets the width of the left margin for an element. Negative values are permitted, but caution is warranted.

Examples:

```
p {margin-left: 5%;}
pre {margin-left: 3em;}
```

Supported by:

Firefox, Internet Explorer, Opera, Safari.

---

margin-right

Values:

<length> | <percentage> | auto | inherit

Initial value:

0

Applies to:

All elements.

Inherited:

No.

Percentages:

Refer to the width of the containing block.

Computed value:

For percentages, as specified; for length values, the absolute length.

Description:

This sets the width of the right margin for an element. Negative values are permitted, but caution is warranted.

Examples:

```
img {margin-right: 30px;}
ol {margin-right: 5em;}
```

Supported by:

Firefox, Internet Explorer, Opera, Safari.

---

margin-top

Values·

<length> | <percentage> | auto | inherit

Initial value:

0

Applies to:

All elements.

Inherited:

No.

Percentages:

Refer to the width of the containing block.

Computed value:

For percentages, as specified; for length values, the absolute length.

Description:

This sets the width of the top margin for an element. Negative values are permitted, but caution is warranted.

Examples:

```
ul {margin-top: 0.5in;}
h3 {margin-top: 1.5em;}
```

Supported by:

Firefox, Internet Explorer, Opera, Safari.

---

max-height

Values:

<length> | <percentage> | none | inherit

Initial value:

Applies to:

All elements except inline nonreplaced elements and table elements.

Inherited:

No.

Percentages:

Refer to the height of the containing block.

Computed value:

For percentages, as specified; for length values, the absolute length; otherwise, none.

Description:

The value of this property sets a maximum constraint on the height of the element. Thus, the element can be shorter than the specified value but not taller. Negative values are not permitted.

Example:

    div#footer {max-height: 3em;}

Supported by:

Firefox, Internet Explorer 7+, Opera, Safari.

max-width

Values:

<length> | <percentage> | none | inherit

Initial value:

Applies to:

All elements except inline nonreplaced elements and table elements.

Inherited:

No.

Percentages:

Refer to the height of the containing block.

Computed value:

For percentages, as specified; for length values, the absolute length; otherwise, none.

Description:

The value of this property sets a maximum constraint on the width of the element. Thus, the element can be narrower than the specified value but not wider. Negative values are not permitted.

Example:

```
#sidebar img {width: 50px; max-width: 100%;}
```

Supported by:

Firefox, Internet Explorer 7+, Opera, Safari.

min-height

Values:

<length> | <percentage> | inherit

Initial value:

0

Applies to:

All elements except inline nonreplaced elements and table elements.

Inherited:

No.

Percentages:

Refer to the width of the containing block.

Computed value:

For percentages, as specified; for length values, the absolute length.

Description:

The value of this property sets a minimum constraint on the height of the element. Thus, the element can be taller than the specified value, but not shorter. Negative values are not permitted.

Example:

```
div#footer {min-height: 1em;}
```

Supported by:

Firefox, Internet Explorer 7+, Opera, Safari.

min-width

Values:

<length> | <percentage> | inherit

Initial value:

0

Applies to:

All elements except inline nonreplaced elements and table elements.

Inherited:

No.

Percentages:

Refer to the width of the containing block.

Computed value:

For percentages, as specified; for length values, the absolute length; otherwise, none.

Description:

The value of this property sets a minimum constraint on the width of the element. Thus, the element can be wider than the specified value, but not narrower. Negative values are not permitted.

Example:

```
div.aside {float: right; width: 13em; max-width: 33%;}
```

Supported by:

Firefox, Internet Explorer 7+, Opera, Safari.

---

outline

Values:

[<outline-color> || <outline-style> || <outline-width>] | inherit

Initial value:

Not defined for shorthand properties.

Applies to:

All elements.

Inherited:

No.

Computed value:

See individual properties (outline-color, etc.).

Description:

This shorthand property is used to set the overall outline for an element. Outlines can be of irregular shape, and they do not change or otherwise affect the placement of elements.

Examples:

```
*[href]:focus {outline: 2px dashed invert;}
form:focus {outline: outset cyan 0.25em;}
```

Supported by:

Firefox, Opera.

---

outline-color

Values:

<color> | invert | inherit

Initial value:

invert (see Description)

Applies to:

All elements.

Inherited:

No.

Computed value:

As specified.

Description:

This property sets the color for the visible portions of the overall outline of an element. Remember that an outline's style must be something other than none for any visible border to appear. User agents are permitted to ignore invert on platforms that don't support color inversion. In that case, the default is the value of color for the element.

Examples:

```
*[href]:focus {outline-color: invert;}
form:focus {outline-color: cyan;}
```

Supported by:

Firefox, Opera.

outline-style

Values:
none | dotted | dashed | solid | double | groove | ridge | inset | outset | inherit

Initial value:
none

Applies to:
All elements

Inherited:
No.

Computed value:
As specified.

Description:
This property is used to set the style for the overall border of an element. The style must be something other than none for any outline to appear.

Examples:
```
*[href]:focus {outline-style: dashed;}
form:focus {outline-style: outset;}
```

Supported by:
Firefox, Opera.

outline-width

Values:
thin | medium | thick | <length> | inherit

Initial value:

Applies to:

All elements.

Inherited:

No.

Computed value:

Absolute length; 0 if the style of the border is none or hidden.

Description:

This property sets the width for the overall outline of an element. The width will take effect only for a given outline if the outline's style is something other than none. If the style is none, then the width is effectively reset to 0. Negative length values are not permitted.

Examples:

```
*[href]:focus {outline-width: 2px;}
form:focus {outline-width: 0.25em;}
```

Supported by:

Firefox, Opera.

---

overflow

Values:

visible | hidden | scroll | auto | inherit

Initial value:

visible

Applies to:

Block-level and replaced elements.

Inherited:

No.

Computed value:

As specified.

Description:

This defines what happens to content that overflows the content area of an element. For the value scroll, user agents should provide a scrolling mechanism whether or not it is actually needed; thus, for example, scrollbars would appear even if all content can fit within the element box.

Examples:

```
#masthead {overflow: hidden;}
object {overflow: scroll;}
```

Supported by:

Firefox, Internet Explorer, Opera, Safari.

Note:

There are layout bugs associated with visible in IE6 and earlier.

---

padding

Values:

[<length> | <percentage>]{1,4} | inherit

Initial value:

Not defined for shorthand elements.

Applies to:

All elements.

Inherited:

No.

Percentages:

Refer to the width of the containing block.

Computed value:

See individual properties (padding-top, etc.).

Note:

Padding can never be negative.

Description:

This shorthand property sets the width of the overall padding for an element or sets the widths of each individual side padding. Padding set on inline nonreplaced elements does not affect line-height calculations; therefore, such an element with both padding and a background may visibly extend into other lines and potentially overlap other content. The background of the element will extend throughout the padding. Negative padding values are not permitted.

Examples:

```
h1 {padding: 2ex;}
img {padding: 10px;}
```

Supported by:

Firefox, Internet Explorer, Opera, Safari.

padding-bottom

Values:

<length> | <percentage> | inherit

Initial value:

0

Applies to:

All elements.

Inherited:

No.

Percentages:

Refer to the width of the containing block.

Computed value:

For percentage values, as specified; for length values, the absolute length.

Note:

Padding can never be negative.

Description:

This property sets the width of the bottom padding for an element. Bottom padding set on inline nonreplaced elements does not affect line-height calculations; therefore, such an element with both bottom padding and a background may visibly extend into other lines and potentially overlap other content. Negative padding values are not permitted.

Examples:

```
ul {padding-bottom: 0.5in;}
h1 {padding-bottom: 2%;}
```

Supported by:

Firefox, Internet Explorer, Opera, Safari.

---

padding-left

Values:

<length> | <percentage> | inherit

Initial value:

0

Applies to:

All elements.

Inherited:

No.

Percentages:

Refer to the width of the containing block.

Computed value:

For percentage values, as specified; for length values, the absolute length.

Note:

Padding can never be negative.

Description:

This property sets the width of the left padding for an element. Left padding set for an inline nonreplaced element will appear only on the left edge of the first inline box generated by the element. Negative padding values are not permitted.

Examples:

```
p {padding-left: 5%;}
pre {padding-left: 3em;}
```

Supported by:

Firefox, Internet Explorer, Opera, Safari.

padding-right

Values:

<length> | <percentage> | inherit

Initial value:

0

Applies to:

All elements.

Inherited:

No.

Percentages:

Refer to the width of the containing block.

Computed value:

For percentage values, as specified; for length values, the absolute length.

Note:

Padding can never be negative.

Description:

This property sets the width of the right padding for an element. Right padding set for an inline nonreplaced element will appear only on the right edge of the last inline box generated by the element. Negative padding values are not permitted.

Examples:

```
img {padding-right: 30px;}
ol {padding-right: 5em;}
```

Supported by:

Firefox, Internet Explorer, Opera, Safari.

padding-top

Values:

<length> | <percentage> | inherit

Initial value:

0

Applies to:

All elements.

Inherited:

No.

Percentages:

Refer to the width of the containing block.

Computed value:

For percentage values, as specified; for length values, the absolute length.

Note:

Padding can never be negative.

Description:

This property sets the width of the top padding for an element. Top padding set on inline nonreplaced elements does not affect line-height calculations; therefore, such an element with both top padding and a background may visibly extend into other lines and potentially overlap other content. Negative padding values are not permitted.

Examples:

```
ul {padding-top: 0.5in;}
h3 {padding-top: 1.5em;}
```

Supported by:

Firefox, Internet Explorer, Opera, Safari.

---

position

Values:

static | relative | absolute | fixed | inherit

Initial value:

static

Applies to:

All elements.

Inherited:

No.

Computed value:

As specified.

Description:

This defines the positioning scheme used to lay out an element. Any element may be positioned, although elements positioned with absolute or fixed will generate a block-level box regardless of what kind of element it is. An element that is relatively positioned is offset from its default placement in the normal flow.

Examples:

```
#footer {position: fixed; bottom: 0;}
*.offset {position: relative; top: 0.5em;}
```

Supported by:

Firefox, Internet Explorer, Opera, Safari.

Note:

Fixed positioning is supported in Explorer only for versions 7 and later.

---

quotes

Values:
[<string> <string>]+ | none | inherit

Initial value:
User agent-dependent.

Applies to:
All elements.

Inherited:
Yes.

Computed value:
As specified.

Description:
This property is used to determine the quotation pattern used with quotes and nested quotes. The actual quote marks are inserted via the property content.

Example:

```
q {quotes: '\201C' '\201D' '\2018' '\2019';}
```

Supported by:

Firefox, Opera.

right

Values:

<length> | <percentage> | auto | inherit

Initial value:

auto

Applies to:

Positioned elements (that is, elements for which the value of position is something other than static).

Inherited:

No.

Percentages:

Refer to the width of the containing block.

Computed value:

For relatively positioned elements, see the following Note; for static elements, auto; for length values, the corresponding absolute length; for percentage values, the specified value; otherwise, auto.

Note:

For relatively positioned elements, the computed value of left always equals right.

Description:

This property defines the offset between the right outer margin edge of a positioned element and the right edge of its containing block.

Examples:

```
div#footer {position: fixed; right: 0;}
*.overlapper {position: relative; right: -25px;}
```

Supported by:

Firefox, Internet Explorer, Opera, Safari.

---

text-align

CSS2.1 values:

left | center | right | justify | inherit

CSS2 values:

left | center | right | justify | <string> | inherit

Initial value:

User agent-specific; may also depend on writing direction.

Applies to:

Block-level elements.

Inherited:

Yes.

Computed value:

As specified.

Note:

CSS2 included a <string> value that was dropped from CSS2.1 due to a lack of support.

Description:

This property sets the horizontal alignment of text within a block-level element by defining the point to which line boxes are aligned. The value justify is supported by allowing user agents to programmatically adjust the word (but not letter) spacing of the line's content; results may vary by user agent.

Examples:

```
p {text-align: justify;}
h4 {text-align: center;}
```

Supported by:

Firefox, Internet Explorer, Opera, Safari.

---

text-decoration

Values:

none | [underline || overline || line-through || blink] | inherit

Initial value:

Applies to:

All elements.

Inherited:

No.

Computed value:

As specified.

Description:

This property allows certain text effects such as underlining. These decorations will span descendant elements that don't have decorations of their own. User agents are not required to support blink. They will span child elements, which do not have text decoration defined; for more details, see Chapter 6 of *CSS: The Definitive Guide*, Third Edition (O'Reilly). Combinations of the values are legal. Any time two text-decoration declarations apply to the same element, the values of the two declarations are *not* combined. For example:

```
h1 {text-decoration: overline;}
h1, h2 {text-decoration: underline;}
```

Given these styles, h1 elements will be underlined with no overline because the value of overline completely overrides the value
of underline. If h1 should have both overlines and underlines, use
the value overline underline for the h1 rule and move it after the
h1, h2 rule; or extend its selector to raise its specificity.

Examples:

```
u {text-decoration: underline;}
.old {text-decoration: line-through;}
u.old {text-decoration: line-through underline;}
```

Supported by:

Firefox, Internet Explorer, Opera, Safari.

Notes:

Explorer does not support the blink value.

There may be inconsistent results regarding text decoration spanning child elements (see Description).

text-indent

Values:

<length> | <percentage> | inherit

Initial value:

0

Applies to:

Block-level elements.

Inherited:

Yes.

Percentages:

Refer to the width of the containing block.

Computed value:

For percentage values, as specified; for length values, the absolute
length.

Description:

This property is used to define the indentation of the first line of content in a block-level element. It is most often used to create a tab effect. Negative values are permitted and cause outdent (or hanging indent) effects.

Examples:

```
p {text-indent: 5em;}
h2 {text-indent: -25px;}
```

Supported by:

Firefox, Internet Explorer, Opera, Safari.

---

text-transform

Values:

uppercase | lowercase | capitalize | none | inherit

Initial value:

Applies to:

All elements.

Inherited:

Yes.

Computed value:

As specified.

Description:

This property changes the case of letters in an element, regardless of the case of the text in the document source. The determination of which letters are to be capitalized by the value capitalize is not precisely defined, as it depends on user agents knowing how to recognize a "word."

Examples:
```
h1 {text-transform: uppercase;}
.title {text-transform: capitalize;}
```

Supported by:

Firefox, Internet Explorer, Opera, Safari.

---

top

Values:

<length> | <percentage> | auto | inherit

Initial value:

auto

Applies to:

Positioned elements (that is, elements for which the value of position is something other than static).

Inherited:

No.

Percentages:

Refer to the height of the containing block.

Computed value:

For relatively positioned elements, see Note; for static elements, auto; for length values, the corresponding absolute length; for percentage values, the specified value; otherwise, auto.

Note:

For relatively positioned elements, if both top and bottom are auto, their computed values are both 0; if one of them is auto, it becomes the negative of the other; if neither is auto, bottom becomes the negative of the value of top.

Description:

This property defines the offset between the top outer margin edge of a positioned element and the top edge of its containing block.

Examples:

```
#masthead {position: fixed; top: 0;}
sub {position: relative; top: 0.5em; vertical-align:
baseline;}
```

Supported by:

Firefox, Internet Explorer, Opera, Safari.

unicode-bidi

Values:

normal | embed | bidi-override | inherit

Initial value:

normal

Applies to:

All elements.

Inherited:

No.

Computed value:

As specified.

Description:

This property allows the author to generate levels of embedding
within the unicode embedding algorithm. User agents that do not
support bidirectional text are permitted to ignore this property.

Examples:

```
*:lang(ar) {direction: rtl; unicode-bidi: embed;}
*:lang(es) {direction: ltr; unicode-bidi: normal;}
```

Supported by:

Firefox, Internet Explorer, Opera 9+.

vertical-align

Values:

baseline | sub | super | top | text-top | middle | bottom | text-bottom | <percentage> | <length> | inherit

Initial value:

baseline

Applies to:

Inline elements and table cells.

Inherited:

No.

Percentages:

Refer to the value of line-height for the element.

Computed value:

For percentage and length values, the absolute length; otherwise, as specified.

Note:

When applied to table cells, only the values baseline, top, middle, and bottom are recognized.

Description:

This defines the vertical alignment of an inline element's baseline with respect to the baseline of the line in which it resides. Negative length and percentage values are permitted, and they lower the element instead of raising it. In table cells, this property sets the alignment of the content of the cell within the cell box.

Examples:

```
sup {vertical-align: super;}
.fnote {vertical-align: 50%;}
```

Supported by:

Firefox, Internet Explorer, Opera, Safari.

visibility

Values:

visible | hidden | collapse | inherit

Initial value:

inherit

Applies to:

All elements.

Inherited:

No.

Computed value:

As specified.

Description:

This specifies whether the element box generated by an element is rendered. This means authors can have the element take up the space it would ordinarily take up, while remaining completely invisible. The value collapse is used in tables to remove columns or rows from the table's layout.

Examples:

```
ul.submenu {visibility: hidden;}
tr.hide {visibility: collapse;}
```

Supported by:

Firefox, Internet Explorer, Opera, Safari.

white-space

Values:

normal | nowrap | pre | pre-wrap | pre-line | inherit

Initial value:

normal

Applies to:

All elements (CSS2.1); block-level elements (CSS2).

Inherited:

No.

Computed value:

As specified.

Description:

This declares how whitespace within an element is handled during layout. normal acts like traditional web browsers, in that it reduces any sequence of whitespace to a single space. pre causes whitespace to be treated as it is in the HTML element pre, with whitespace and returns fully preserved. nowrap prevents an element from line-breaking, as in the "nowrap" attribute for td and th elements in HTML4. The values pre-wrap and pre-line were added in CSS2.1; the former causes the user agent to preserve whitespace while still automatically wrapping lines of text, and the latter honors newline characters within the text while collapsing all other whitespace as per normal.

Examples:

```
td {white-space: nowrap;}
tt {white-space: pre;}
```

Supported by:

Firefox, Internet Explorer, Opera, Safari.

Note:

As of this writing, pre-wrap is supported only by Opera 8 and later, whereas pre-line has no known support.

---

width

Values:

<length> | <percentage> | auto | inherit

Initial value:

auto

Applies to:

Block-level and replaced elements.

Inherited:

No.

Percentages:

Refer to the width of the containing block.

Computed value:

For auto and percentage values, as specified; otherwise, an absolute length, unless the property does not apply to the element (then auto).

Description:

This defines the width of an element's content area, outside of which padding, borders, and margins are added. This property is ignored for inline nonreplaced elements. Negative length and percentage values are not permitted.

Examples:

```
table {width: 80%;}
#sidebar {width: 20%;}
.figure img {width: 200px;}
```

Supported by:

Firefox, Internet Explorer, Opera, Safari.

Note:

In IE6 and earlier, width is treated as a minimum width, not a fixed width.

word-spacing

Values:
<length> | normal | inherit

Initial value:
normal

Applies to:
All elements.

Inherited:
Yes.

Computed value:
For normal, the absolute length 0; otherwise, the absolute length.

Description:
This defines the amount of whitespace to be inserted between words in an element. For the purposes of this property, a word is defined to be a string of characters surrounded by whitespace. Length values create a modifier to the usual spacing between words; thus, normal is synonymous with 0. Negative length values are permitted and will cause words to bunch closer together.

Examples:
```
p.spacious {word-spacing: 0.5em;}
em {word-spacing: 5px;}
p.cramped {word-spacing: -0.2em;}
```

Supported by:
Firefox, Internet Explorer, Opera, Safari.

z-index

Values:
<integer> | auto | inherit

Initial value:
auto

Applies to:
Positioned elements.

Inherited:
No.

Computed value:
As specified.

Description:
This property sets the placement of a positioned element along the z-axis, which is defined to be the axis that extends perpendicular to the display area. Positive numbers are closer to the user, and negative numbers are further away.

Example:
```
#masthead {position: relative; z-index: 10000;}
```

Supported by:
Firefox, Internet Explorer, Opera, Safari.

Tables

border-collapse

Values:
collapse | separate | inherit

Initial value:
separate

Applies to:
Elements with the display value table or table-inline.

Inherited:
Yes.

Computed value:
As specified.

Note:
In CSS2, the default value was collapse.

Description:
This property is used to define the layout model used in laying out the borders in a table—i.e., those applied to cells, rows, and so forth. Although the property applies only to tables, it is inherited by all the elements within the table.

Example:
```
table {border-collapse: separate; border-spacing: 3px
5px;}
```

Supported by:
Firefox, Opera, Safari.

border-spacing

Values:

<length> <length>? | inherit

Initial value:

0

Applies to:

Elements with the display value table or table-inline.

Inherited:

Yes.

Computed value:

Two absolute lengths.

Note:

Property is ignored unless the border-collapse value is separate.

Description:

This specifies the distance between cell borders in the separated borders model. The first of the two length values is the horizontal separation and the second is the vertical. This property is ignored unless border-collapse is set to separate. Although the property applies only to tables, it is inherited by all of the elements within the table.

Examples:

```
table {border-collapse: separate; border-spacing: 0;}
table {border-collapse: separate; border-spacing: 3px
5px;}
```

Supported by:

Firefox, Internet Explorer, Opera, Safari.

caption-side

Values:
top | bottom

Initial value:
top

Applies to:
Elements with the display value table-caption.

Inherited:
No.

Computed value:
As specified.

Note:
The values left and right appeared in CSS2 but were dropped from CSS2.1 due to a lack of widespread support.

Description:
This specifies the placement of a table caption with respect to the table box. The caption is rendered as though it were a block-level element placed just before (or after) the table.

Example:
```
caption {caption-side: top;}
```

Supported by:
Firefox, Internet Explorer 7+, Opera, Safari.

Note:
Only Firefox supports the left and right values.

empty-cells

Values:

show | hide | inherit

Initial value:

show

Applies to:

Elements with the display value table-cell.

Inherited:

Yes.

Computed value:

As specified.

Note:

Property is ignored unless the border-collapse value is separate.

Description:

This defines the presentation of table cells that contain no content. If shown, the cell's borders and background are drawn. This property is ignored unless border-collapse is set to separate.

Example:

    th, td {empty-cells: show;}

Supported by:

Firefox, Internet Explorer, Opera, Safari.

Note:

Explorer's support appears to apply only to entire rows of hidden cells and not to empty cells in a row of nonempty cells.

table-layout

Values:

auto | fixed | inherit

Initial value:

auto

Applies to:

Elements with the display value table or inline-table.

Inherited:

Yes.

Computed value:

As specified.

Description:

This property is used to specify which layout algorithm is used to lay out a table. The fixed layout algorithm is faster but less flexible, whereas the automatic algorithm is slower but more reflective of traditional HTML tables.

Example:

    table.fast {table-layout: fixed;}

Supported by:

None.

Paged Media

orphans

Values:
<integer> | inherit

Initial value:
2

Applies to:
Block-level elements.

Inherited:
Yes.

Computed value:
As specified.

Description:
This specifies the minimum number of text lines within the element that can be left at the bottom of a page. This can affect the placement of page breaks within the element.

Examples:
```
p {orphans: 4;}
ul {orphans: 2;}
```

Supported by:
Unknown.

page-break-after

Values:

auto | always | avoid | left | right | inherit

Initial value:

auto

Applies to:

Nonfloated block-level elements with a position value of relative or static.

Inherited:

No.

Computed value:

As specified.

Description:

This declares whether page breaks should be placed after an element. Although it is theoretically possible to force breaks with always, it is not possible to guarantee prevention; avoid asks the user agent to avoid inserting a page break if possible.

Examples:

```
div.section {page-break-after: always;}
h2 {page-break-after: avoid;}
```

Supported by:

Firefox, Internet Explorer, Opera, Safari.

Note:

The behavior of this property is highly unpredictable and may be buggy in some or all browsers listed.

page-break-before

Values:

auto | always | avoid | left | right | inherit

Initial value:

auto

Applies to:

Nonfloated block-level elements with a position value of relative or static.

Inherited:

No.

Computed value:

As specified.

Description:

Declares whether page breaks should be placed before an element. Although it is theoretically possible to force breaks with always, it is not possible to guarantee prevention; the best an author can do is ask the user agent to avoid inserting a page break if possible.

Examples:

```
p + ul {page-break-before: avoid;}
h2 {page-break-before: always;}
```

Supported by:

Firefox, Internet Explorer, Opera, Safari.

Note:

The behavior of this property is highly unpredictable and may be buggy in some or all browsers listed.

page-break-inside

Values:

auto | avoid | inherit

Initial value:

auto

Applies to:

Nonfloated block-level elements with a position value of relative or static.

Inherited:

Yes.

Computed value:

As specified.

Description:

This declares whether page breaks should be placed inside an element. Because an element might be taller than a page box, it is not possible to guarantee prevention; the best an author can do is ask the user agent to avoid inserting a page break if possible.

Example:

```
table {page-break-inside: avoid;}
```

Supported by:

Firefox, Opera, Safari.

Note:

The behavior of this property is highly unpredictable and may be buggy in some or all browsers listed.

widows

Values:

<integer> | inherit

Initial value:

2

Applies to:

Block-level elements.

Inherited:

Yes.

Computed value:

As specified.

Description:

This specifies the minimum number of text lines within the element that can be left at the top of a page. This can affect the placement of page breaks within the element.

Examples:

```
p {widows: 4;}
ul {widows: 2;}
```

Supported by:

Unknown.

Dropped from CSS2.1

The following properties appeared in CSS2 but were dropped from CSS2.1 due to a lack of widespread support. They do not have computed value information because computed values were first explicitly defined in CSS2.1.

Visual Styles

font-size-adjust

Values:

<number> | none | inherit

Initial value:

Applies to:

All elements.

Inherited:

Yes.

Description:

The aim of this property is to allow authors to trigger font scaling such that substitute fonts will not look too wildly different from the font the author wanted to use, even if the substituted font has a different x-height. Note that this property does not appear in CSS2.1. As of this writing, only Firefox for Windows supports it.

font-stretch

Values:

normal | wider | narrower | ultra-condensed | extra-condensed | condensed | semi-condensed | semi-expanded | expanded | extra-expanded | ultra-expanded | inherit

Initial value:

normal

Applies to:

All elements.

Inherited:

Yes.

Description:

With this property, the character glyphs in a given font can be made wider or narrower, ideally by selected condensed or expanded faces from the font's family. Note that this property does not appear in CSS2.1.

---

marker-offset

Values:

<length> | auto | inherit

Initial value:

auto

Applies to:

Elements with a display value of marker.

Inherited:

No.

Note:

This property is obsolete as of CSS2.1 and will likely not appear in CSS3, with the same holding true for the display value of marker; as of this writing, it appears that other mechanisms will be used to achieve these effects.

Description:

This property specifies the distance between the nearest border edge of a marker box and its associated element box.

---

text-shadow

Values:

none | [<color> || <length> <length> <length>? ,]* [<color> || <length> <length> <length>?] | inherit

Initial value:

Applies to:

All elements.

Inherited:

No.

Description:

This permits the assignments of one or more "shadows" to the text in an element. The first two length values in a shadow definition set horizontal and vertical offsets, respectively, from the element's text. The third length defines a blurring radius. Note that this property does not appear in CSS2.1. As of this writing, Safari supports text-shadow but restricts the value to a single shadow.

Paged Media

marks

Values:

[crop || cross] | none | inherit

Initial value:

Applies to:

Page context.

Inherited:

N/A.

Description:

This property defines whether "cross marks" (otherwise known as register marks or registration marks) should be placed outside the content area but within the printable area of the canvas. The exact placement and rendering of the marks is not defined. Note that this property does not appear in CSS2.1.

---

page

Values:
<identifier> | inherit

Initial value:
auto

Applies to:
Block-level elements.

Inherited:
Yes.

Description:
This property, in conjunction with size, specifies a particular page type to be used in the printing of an element. Note that this property does not appear in CSS2.1.

---

size

Values:
<length>{1,2} | auto | portrait | landscape | inherit

Initial value:
auto

Applies to:
The page area.

Inherited:
No.

Description:
With this property, authors can declare the size and orientation of the page box used in the printing of an element. It can be used in conjunction with page, although that is not always necessary. Note that this property does not appear in CSS2.1.

Aural Styles

azimuth

Values:

<angle> | [[left-side | far-left | left | center-left | center |
center-right | right | far-right | right-side] || behind] |
leftwards | rightwards | inherit

Initial value:

center

Applies to:

All elements.

Inherited:

Yes.

Computed value:

Normalized angle.

Description:

This property sets the angle along the horizontal plane (otherwise
known as the horizon) from which a sound should seem to
emanate. It is used in conjunction with elevation to place the
sound at a point on a hypothetical sphere with the user at its
center.

Supported by:

Emacspeak.

cue

Values:

[<cue-before> || <cue-after>] | inherit

Initial value:

Applies to:

All elements.

Inherited:

No.

Computed value:

See individual properties (cue-before, etc.).

Description:

This is a shorthand property that allows an author to define cues that precede and follow the audio rendering of an element's content. A cue is something like an auditory icon.

Supported by:

Emacspeak.

cue-after

Values:

<uri> | none | inherit

Initial value:

Applies to:

All elements.

Inherited:

No.

Computed value:

For <uri> values, the absolute URI; otherwise, none.

Description:

This property allows an author to define a cue that follows the audio rendering of an element's content.

Supported by:

Emacspeak.

---

cue-before

Values:

<uri> | none | inherit

Initial value:

Applies to:

All elements.

Inherited:

No.

Computed value:

For <uri> values, the absolute URI; otherwise, none.

Description:

This property allows an author to define a cue that precedes the audio rendering of an element's content.

Supported by:

Emacspeak.

---

elevation

Values:

<angle> | below | level | above | higher | lower | inherit

Initial value:

level

Applies to:

All elements.

Inherited:

Yes.

Computed value:

Normalized angle.

Description:

This property sets the angle above or below the horizontal plane (otherwise known as the horizon) from which a sound should seem to emanate. This is used in conjunction with azimuth to place the sound at a point on a hypothetical sphere with the user at its center.

Supported by:

Emacspeak.

---

pause

Values:

[[<time> | <percentage>]{1,2}] | inherit

Initial value:

0

Applies to:

All elements.

Inherited:

No.

Computed value:

See individual properties (pause-before, etc.).

Description:

This is a shorthand property that allows an author to define pauses that precede and follow the audio rendering of an element's content. A pause is an interval in which no content is audibly rendered, although background sounds may still be audible.

Supported by:

Emacspeak.

---

pause-after

Values:

<time> | <percentage> | inherit

Initial values:

0

Applies to:

All elements.

Inherited:

No.

Computed value:

The absolute time value.

Description:

This property allows an author to define the length of a pause that follows the audio rendering of an element's content.

Supported by:

Emacspeak.

---

pause-before

Values:

<time> | <percentage> | inherit

Initial value:

0

Applies to:

All elements.

Inherited:

No.

Computed value:

The absolute time value.

Description:

This property allows an author to define the length of a pause that precedes the audio rendering of an element's content.

Supported by:

Emacspeak.

pitch

Values:

<frequency> | x-low | low | medium | high | x-high | inherit

Initial value:

medium

Applies to:

All elements.

Inherited:

Yes.

Computed value:

The absolute frequency value.

Description:

This property specifies the average pitch (frequency) of the speaking voice used to audibly render the element's content. The average pitch of a voice will depend greatly on the voice family.

Supported by:

Emacspeak.

pitch-range

Values:

<number> | inherit

Initial value:

50

Applies to:

All elements.

Inherited:

Yes.

Computed value:

As specified.

Description:

This property specifies the variation in average pitch used by the speaking voice, while audibly rendering the element's content. The higher the variation, the more animated the voice will sound.

Supported by:

Emacspeak.

play-during

Values:

<uri> | [mix || repeat]? | auto | none | inherit

Initial value:

auto

Applies to:

All elements.

Inherited:

No.

Computed value:

For <uri> values, the absolute URI; otherwise, as specified.

Description:

This provides a sound to be played in the background while the element's contents are audibly rendered. The sound can be mixed with other background sounds (set using play-during on an ancestor element), or it can replace other sounds for the duration of the element's audio rendering.

Supported by:

Emacspeak.

richness

Values:

<number> | inherit

Initial value:

50

Applies to:

All elements.

Inherited:

Yes.

Computed value:

As specified.

Description:

This property sets the brightness of the speaking voice used when audibly rendering the element's content. The brighter the voice, the more it will carry.

Supported by:

Emacspeak.

---

speak

Values:

normal | none | spell-out | inherit

Initial value:

normal

Applies to:

All elements.

Inherited:

Yes.

Computed value:

As specified.

Description:

This determines how an element's contents will be audibly rendered or whether they will be rendered at all. The value spell-out is typically used for acronyms and abbreviations, such as W3C or CSS. If the value is none, the element is skipped (it takes no time to be audibly rendered).

Supported by:

Emacspeak.

---

speak-header

Values:

once | always | inherit

Initial value:

once

Applies to:

Elements containing table header information.

Inherited:

Yes.

Computed value:

As specified.

Description:

This specifies whether the content of table headers is spoken before every cell associated with those headers or only when the header associated with a cell is different than the header associated with the previously rendered cell.

Supported by:

Emacspeak

speak-numeral

Values:

digits | continuous | inherit

Initial value:

continuous

Applies to:

All elements.

Inherited:

Yes.

Computed value:

As specified.

Description:

This property determines how numbers are spoken during audible rendering.

Supported by:

Emacspeak.

---

speak-punctuation

Values:

code | none | inherit

Initial value:

Applies to:

All elements.

Inherited:

Yes.

Computed value:

As specified.

Description:

This property determines how punctuation is spoken during audible rendering. The value code causes punctuation symbols to be rendered literally.

Supported by:

Emacspeak.

---

speech-rate

Values:

<number> | x-slow | slow | medium | fast | x-fast | faster| slower | inherit

Initial value:

medium

Applies to:

All elements.

Inherited:

Yes.

Computed value:

An absolute number.

Description:

This sets the average rate at which words are spoken when an element's content is audibly rendered.

Supported by:

Emacspeak.

stress

Values:

<number> | inherit

Initial value:

50

Applies to:

All elements.

Inherited:

Yes.

Computed value:

As specified.

Description:

This property affects the height of peaks in the intonation of a speaking voice, which are in turn generated by stress marks within a language.

Supported by:

Emacspeak.

voice-family

Values:

[[<specific-voice> | <generic-voice>],]* [<specific-voice> | <generic-voice>] | inherit

Initial value:

User agent-dependent.

Applies to:

All elements.

Inherited:

Yes.

Computed value:

As specified.

Description:

This property is used to define a list of voice families that can be used in the audio rendering of an element's content and is comparable to font-family. The permitted generic voices are male, female, and child.

Supported by:

Emacspeak.

---

volume

Values:

<number> | <percentage> | silent | x-soft | soft | medium | loud | x-loud | inherit

Initial value:

medium

Applies to:

All elements.

Inherited:

Yes.

Computed value:

An absolute number.

Description:

This sets the median volume level for the waveform of the audibly rendered content. Thus, a waveform with large peaks and valleys may go well above or below the volume level set with this property. Note that 0 is not the same as silent.

Supported by:

Emacspeak.

Index

We'd like to hear your suggestions for improving our indexes. Send email to
index@oreilly.com.

X

x-height (ex), 32
x-height relative length value, 32
xml-stylesheet processing
    instruction, 5

Z

z-index property, 125

ISBN	Title	Author	Year	Price

Shroff / O'Reilly

TITLES AT REDUCED PRICES

ISBN	Title	Author	Year	Price
8173663661	.NET Framework Essentials, *324 Pages*	Thai	2002	25.00
8173665753	802.11 Security, *200 Pages*	Potter	2003	50.00
9788184040272	Access 2003 for Starters: The Missing Manual, *408 Pages*	Chase	2005	75.00
8173664277	Access Cookbook for 97, 2000 & 2002 **(Book / CD-ROM)**, *724 Pages*	Getz	2002	100.00
8173667446	Apache Cookbook (Covers Apache 2.0 & 1.3), *264 Pages*	Coar	2003	75.00
9788184040012	Asterisk: The Future of Telephony, *414 Pages*	Meggelen	2005	50.00
8173662886	Building Oracle XML Applications **(Book / CD-ROM)**, *824 Pgs*	Muench	2000	100.00
8173665621	Building Secure Servers with Linux, *454 Pages*	Bauer	2003	100.00
8173664250	Building Wireless Community Networks, *144 Pages*	Flickenger	2002	50.00
8173662584	Cascading Style Sheets: The Definitive Guide, *476 Pages*	Meyer	2000	75.00
8173669066	Cascading Style Sheets: The Definitive Guide (Covers CSS2 & CSS 2.1), 2/ed, *538 Pages*	Meyer	2004	100.00
8173667241	Cisco Cookbook, *918 Pages*	Dooley	2003	150.00
8173669163	CSS Cookbook (Cover CSS 2.1), *280 Pages*	Schmitt	2004	75.00
8173663882	Designing Large Scale LANs, *408 Pages*	Dooley	2002	75.00
8173662878	Developing ASP Components 2/ed, *864 Pages*	Powers	1998	100.00
817366272X	DHCP for Windows 2000, *288 Pages*	Alcott	2001	75.00
8173665281	Dynamic HTML: The Definitive Reference, 2/ed, *1,428 Pages*	Goodman	2006	150.00
8173669430	Essentail SharePoint, *338 Pages*	Webb	2005	50.00
8173663580	Essential SNMP, *338 Pages*	Mauro	2001	75.00
8173662754	Excel 2000 In a Nutshell: A Power User's Quick Reference, *560 Pages*	Simon	2000	50.00
8173669406	Excel Annoyances: How to Fix the Most Annoying Things about Your Favorite Spreadsheet , *266 Pages*	Frye	2004	75.00
8173668612	Excel Hacks: 100 Industrial Strength Tips & Tools, *316 Pages*	David	2004	75.00
8173663599	Exim: The Mail Transport Agent, *638 Pages*	Hazel	2001	75.00
817366949X	Google Hacks: Tips & Tools for Smarter Searching 2/ed, *496 Pages*	Calishain	2005	100.00
8173669325	Google: The Missing Manual, *312 Pages*	Milstein	2004	75.00
8173665109	Information Architecture for the World Wide Web, 2/ed, *492 Pages*	Rosenfeld	2002	100.00
817366448X	IPv6 Essentials, *362 Pages*	Hagen	2002	75.00
9788173660573	Java Threads, 2/ed, *336 Pages*	Oaks	1999	100.00
8173664625	Java Enterprise in a Nutshell: A Desktop Quick Reference, 2/ed, *1,004 Pages*	Farley	2002	100.00
9788173660559	Java Foundation Classes in a Nutshell, *752 Pages*	Flanagan	1999	75.00
8173662711	Java Internationalization, *456 Pages*	Deitsch	1998	75.00
8173663807	Java Programming with Oracle SQLJ, *404 Pages*	Price	2001	75.00
8173661103	JavaScript Application Cookbook, *512 Pages*	Bradenbaugh	1999	75.00
8173666709	JavaScript and DHTML Cookbook, *546 Pages*	Goodman	2003	75.00
8173661111	JavaScript Pocket Reference, *96 Pages*	Flanagan	1998	25.00
8173662509	Jini in a Nutshell, *420 Pages*	Oaks	2000	75.00
8173665168	Learning C#, *374 Pages*	Liberty	2002	75.00
8173663173	Learning WML & WMLScript, *204 Pages*	Frost	2002	50.00
8173663602	Linux Device Drivers, 2/ed, *650 Pages*	Rubini	2002	150.00
8173662568	Lotus Domino in a Nutshell, *370 Pages*	Neilson	2000	50.00
8173662746	Managing IMAP, *412 Pages*	Mullet	2000	50.00
8173663610	Managing NFS & NIS, 2/ed, *518 Pages*	Stern	2001	100.00
8173665087	Mastering Regular Expressions, 2/ed, *492 Pages*	Friedl	2002	150.00
8173662193	MCSD in a Nutshell: The Visual Basic Exams, *636 Pages*	Foxall	2000	75.00
8173662398	MCSE in a Nutshell: The Windows 2000 Exams, *504 Pages*	Moncur	1998	75.00

ISBN	Title	Author	Year	Price
8173666776	MySQL Pocket Reference, 94 Pages	Reese	2003	25.00
8173665648	MySQL Cookbook (Covers MySQL 4.0), 1,028 Pages	DuBois	2003	150.00
8173663521	Network Security Hacks: 100 Industrial-Strength Tips & Tools, 328 Pages	Lockhart	2004	100.00
8173665613	Object-Oriented Programming with Visual Basic .NET, 306 Pages	Hamilton	2003	50.00
8173664110	Oracle Essentials: Oracle9i, Oracle8i & Oracle8, 2/ed, 382 Pages	Greenwald	2001	50.00
817366935X	Oracle Essentials: Oracle Database 10g, 3/ed, 368 Pages	Greenwald	2004	100.00
8173663629	Oracle PL/SQL Best Practices, 208 Pages	Feuerstein	2001	50.00
9788184042542	Oracle PL/SQL Language Pocket Reference, 3/ed, 140 Pages	Feuerstein	2006	25.00
8173663246	Oracle Net8 Configuration & Troubleshooting, 412 Pages	Toledo	1998	75.00
8173668027	PC Annoyances: How to Fix the Most Annoying Thingsabout your Personal Computer, 236 Pages	Bass	2003	75.00
8173661227	Perl 5 Pocket Reference, 2/ed, 96 Pages	Vromans	2002	25.00
9788173667190	Perl 6 Essentials, 208 Pages	Randal	2003	75.00
8173661243	Perl/Tk Pocket Reference, 104 Pages	Lidie	1998	25.00
8173665710	PHP Cookbook, 638 Pages	Sklar	2003	150.00
817366269X	PHP Pocket Reference, 124 Pages	Lerdorf	2000	25.00
817366126X	Practical Internet Groupware, 520 Pages	Udell	1999	75.00
8173666857	Python in a Nutshell: A Desktop Quick Reference (Cover Python 2.2), 662 Pages	Martelli	2006	75.00
817366711X	Practical mod_perl, 932 Pages	Bekman	2003	150.00
8173666733	Practical RDF, 360 Pages	Powers	2003	100.00
8173667500	Programming Python (Covers Python 2) 2/ed, (Book / CD-ROM), 1,322 Pages	Lutzf	2001	150.00
817366207X	Programming Web Services with XML-RPC, 240 Pages	St.Laurent	2001	50.00
8173660190	QuarkXPress in a Nutshell, 552 Pages	O'Quinn	1998	50.00
8173664226	SAX2 (Simple API for XML), 248 Pages	Brownell	2002	50.00
8173663262	Securing Windows NT/2000 Servers for the Internet, 200 Pages	Norberg	1998	50.00
8173662487	sed & awk Pocket Reference, 60 Pages	Robbins	1998	25.00
8173661294	sendmail Desktop Reference, 74 Pages	Costales	1997	25.00
8173665834	sendmail, 3/ed, 1,238 Pages	Costales	2002	150.00
8173664161	Server Load Balancing, 198 Pages	Bourke	2001	50.00
8173663866	Solaris 8 Administrator's Guide, 308 Pages	Watters	2002	100.00
8173662924	SSH: The Secure Shell: The Definitive Guide, 564 Pages	Barrett	2001	75.00
8173663254	T1: A Survival Guide, 312 Pages	Gast	2001	50.00
8173666873	Tomcat: The Definitive Guide (Cover Tomcat 4), 336 Pages	Brittain	2004	100.00
8173662606	Tcl/Tk Pocket Reference, 100 Pages	Raines	1998	25.00
8173664374	VB .NET Core Classes in a Nutshell: A Desktop Quick Reference (Book / CD-ROM), 584 Pages	Kurniawan	2002	75.00
8173663300	VBScript Pocket Reference, 118 Pages	Childs	2000	25.00
817366501X	Visual Studio Hacks: Tips & Tools for Turbocharging the IDE, 304 Pages	Avery	2005	75.00
9788173663475	Web Database Applications with PHP & MySQL, 600 Pages	Williams	2002	75.00
8173665931	WebLogic Server 6.1 Workbook for Enterprise JavaBeans, 3/ed, 264 Pages	Nyberg	2001	50.00
8173661359	Webmaster in a Nutshell, 2/ed, 540 Pages	Spainhour	1999	75.00
8173662630	Windows 2000 Active Directory, 624 Pages	Lowe-Norris	2002	75.00
8173662789	Windows 2000 Administration in a Nutshell: A Desktop Quick Reference, 1,000 Pages	Tulloch	2001	50.00
8173663327	Windows 2000 Performance Guide, 650 Pages	Friedman	2002	75.00
9788173660740	Windows 2000 Quick Fixes, 304 Pages	Boyce	2001	50.00
8173666903	Windows Server 2003 in a Nutshell: A Desktop Quick Reference, 672 Pages	Tulloch	2003	75.00
8173663564	Windows XP in a Nutshell: A Desktop Quick Reference, 640 Pages	Karp	2002	75.00
8173665915	Windows XP Unwired: A Guide for Home, Office, and the Road, 316 Pages	Lee	2003	75.00
8173667462	Wireless Hacks: 100 Industrial-Strength Tips & Tools, 424 Pages	Flickenger	2003	100.00
8173662770	Word 2000 in a Nutshell: A Power User's Quick Reference, 516 Pages	Glenn	2000	50.00
8173666113	Word Annoyances, 218 Pages	Hart	2005	75.00
8173668094	Xlib Programming Manual (Version 11): Volume One, 824 Pages	Nye	1994	100.00
8173668108	Xlib Reference Manual (Version 11), 3/ed: Volume Two, 948 Pages	Nye	1994	100.00
8173668086	X Protocol Reference Manual (Version X11): Volume Zero, 468 Pages	Nye	1995	75.00

ISBN	Title	Author	Year	Price
8173660778	Writing Word Macros, *416 Pages*	Roman	1998	50.00

PUBLISHED TITLES

ISBN	Title	Author	Year	Price
9788184046892	97 Things Every Software Architect Should Know, *236 Pages*	Monson	2009	300.00
8173666539	.NET and XML, *484 Pages*	Bornstein	2004	425.00
8173669201	.NET Compact Framework Pocket Guide, *122 Pages*	Lee	2004	125.00
8173665729	.NET Gotchas: 75 Ways to Improve Your C# and VB.NET Programs, *402 Pages*	Subramaniam	2005	300.00
9788184041637	802.11 Wireless Networks: The Definitive Guide, 2nd Edition (Covers 802.11a, g, n & i), *668 Pages*	Gast	2005	550.00
9788184043099	A+, Network+, Security+ Exams in a Nutshell (Cover Essentials 220-602,220-603,220-604 N10-00, *826 Pages*	Bhardwaj	2007	600.00
8173661995	Access 2003 Personal Trainer (**Book / CD-ROM**), (2 Color book), *372 Pages*	CustomGuide	2005	400.00
9788184042573	Access 2007: The Missing Manual, *776 Pages*	MacDonald	2006	525.00
9788184042924	Access 2007 For Starters: The Missing Manual, *426 Pages*	MacDonald	2007	375.00
9788184043334	Access Data Analysis Cookbook, *384 Pages*	Bluttman	2007	375.00
9788173664281	Access Database Design & Programming, 3/ed, *454 Pages*	Roman	2002	325.00
8173666372	Access Hacks: Tips & Tools for Wrangling Your Data, *362 Pages*	Bluttman	2005	325.00
9788184042832	ActionScript 3.0 Cookbook, *600 Pages*	Lott	2006	475.00
9788173667237	ActionScript Cookbook, *904 Pages*	Lott	2003	675.00
9788184043747	ActionScript 3.0 Design Patterns: Object Oriented Programming Techniques (Adobe Developer Library), *546 Pages*	Sanders	2007	450.00
9788184046120	ActionScript 3.0 Quick Reference Guide, The, *508 Pages*	Stiller	2008	425.00
8173666555	ActionScript for Flash MX Pocket Reference, *152 Pages*	Moock	2003	125.00
8173665761	ActionScript for Flash MX: The Definitive Guide, 2/ed, *904 Pages*	Colin Moock	2003	750.00
8184046496496	Active Directory: Designing, Deploying, and Running Active Directory, 4/ed, *876 Pages*	Desmond	2008	800.00
8173667357	Active Directory Cookbook for Windows Server 2003 and Windows 2000, *632 Pages*	Allen	1993	525.00
8173666563	Active Directory for Windows Server 2003, 2/ed, *692 Pages*	Allen	2003	575.00
9788184047103	Active Directory Cookbook, 3/ed:Solutions for Administrators & Developers, *1104 Pages*	Hunter	2009	750.00
9788184045390	Adobe AIR for JavaScript Developers Pocket Guide, *220 Pages*	Chambers	2008	150.00
9788184043501	Adding Ajax, *418 Pages*	Power	2007	400.00
9788184044980	ADO.NET 3.5 Cookbook, 2/ed (Updated for .NET 3.5, LINQ, and SQL Server 2008), *1,098 Pages*	Hamilton	2008	750.00
8184046446441	Adobe AIR 1.5 Cookbook: Solutions and Examples for Rich Internet Application Developers, *460 Pages*	Tucker	2008	500.00
9788184043563	Adobe Integrated Runtime(AIR) for JavaScript Developers Pocket Reference, *192 Pages*	Dura	2007	150.00
9788173668302	Advanced Perl Programming, 2/ed, *308 Pages*	Cozens	2005	325.00
9788184044409	Advanced Rails, *374 Pages*	Ediger	2008	375.00
8173668205	AI for Game Developers, *400 Pages*	Bourg	2004	375.00
9788184046083	Algorithms in a Nutshell: A Desktop Quick Reference, *376 Pgs*	Heineman	2008	250.00
9788184041576	Ajax Design Patterns, *668 Pages*	Mahemoff	2006	500.00
9788184041064	Ajax Hacks: Tips & Tools for Creating Responsive Web Sites, *304 Pgs*	Perry	2006	350.00
9788184043082	Ajax on Java, *176 Pages*	Olson	2007	250.00
9788184042610	Ajax on Rails, *364 Pages*	Raymond	2007	350.00
9788184044898	Ajax: The Definitive Guide, *996 Pages*	Holdener	2008	750.00
8173667262	Amazon Hacks: 100 Industrial Strength Tips & Tricks, *312 Pages*	Bausch	2003	250.00
8173667799	Analyzing Business Data with Excel, *276 Pages*	Knight	2006	275.00
9788184040807	ANT: The Definitive Guide, 2/ed (Cover ANT 1.6), *346 Pages*	Holzner	2005	375.00
9788184044416	Apache Cookbook, 2/ed, *322 Pages*	Bowen	2008	375.00
8173662525	Apache Pocket Reference, *112 Pages*	Ford	2000	75.00
9788184046007	Apache 2 Pocket Reference, *230 Pages*	Ford	2008	150.00
8173662274	Apache Security, *428 Pages*	Ristic	2005	400.00
8173665133	Apache: The Definitive Guide (Covers Apache 2.0 & 1.3) 3/ed, *594 Pages*	Laurie	2002	500.00
9788184043549	Apollo for Adobe Flex Developers Pocket Guide, *154 Pages*	Dixon	2007	125.00
9788184040395	Applied Software Project Management, *304 Pages*	Stellman	2005	350.00
9788184044232	The Art of Agile Development, *446 Pages*	Shore	2007	450.00

ISBN	Title	Author	Year	Price
9788184045963	**The Art of Capacity Planning, 168 Pages**	**Allspaw**	**2008**	**200.00**
9788173667831	The Art of Project Management, *512 Pages*	Berkun	2005	350.00
9788184041415	The Art of SQL, *382 Pages*	Faroult	2006	400.00
9788184041026	ASP .NET 2.0 Cookbook (Cover ASP .NET 2.0), *1,028 Pages*	Kittel	2005	675.00
8173664587	ASP .NET 2.0: Developer's Notebook, *358 Pages*	Lee	2005	325.00
8173669384	AspectJ Cookbook, *364 Pages*	Miles	2004	350.00
9788184045468	**Asterisk: The Future of Telephony, 2/ed, 618 Pages**	**Meggelen**	**2008**	**575.00**
9788184042702	Astronomy Hacks, *420 Pages*	Thompson	2005	450.00
8173662347	AutoCAD 2000 In a Nutshell: A Command Reference Guide, *592 Pages*	Kent	1999	325.00
9788184042900	**BacKup & Recovery, 774 Pages**	**Preston**	**2007**	**600.00**
9788184043471	**Bash Cookbook, 640 Pages**	**Albing**	**2007**	**500.00**
9788184043556	**Beautiful Code: Leading Programmers Explain How**			
	They Think, 634 Pages	**Wilson**	**2007**	**500.00**
9788184046908	**Beautiful Architecture, 442 Pages**	**Gousios**	**2009**	**500.00**
9788184047110	**Beautiful Security, 316 Pages**	**Oram**	**2009**	**350.00**
9788184047035	**Beautiful Teams, 524 Pages**	**Stellman**	**2009**	**475.00**
9788173663956	Beginning Perl for Bioinformatics, *390 Pages*	Tisdall	2001	350.00
8173668981	Better, Faster, Lighter Java, *270 Pages*	Tate	2004	250.00
9788184000036	Beyond Java, *206 Pages*	Tate	2005	200.00
9788173666582	BGP, *292 Pages*	van Beijnum	2002	275.00
9788184040548	Blackberry Hacks: Tips & Tools for Your Mobile Office, *350 Pages*	Mabe	2005	350.00
8173665125	BLAST, *372 Pages*	Korf	2003	325.00
817366899X	BSD Hacks:100 Industrial-Strength Tips & Tools, *458 Pages*	Lavigne	2004	375.00
9788184044393	**Building a Web 2.0 Portal with ASP.NET 3.5, 324 Pages**	**Zabir**	**2008**	**325.00**
9788173666599	Building Embedded Linux Systems, *422 Pages*	Yaghmour	2003	350.00
9788184047127	**Building Embedded Linux Systems, 2/ed:**			
	Concepts, techniques, tricks, and traps, *478 Pages*	Gerum	2009	450.00
8173661014	Building Internet Firewalls 2/ed, *904 Pages*	Chapman	2000	650.00
8173662282	Building Java Enterprise Applications: Vol. 1 - Architecture, *324 Pgs*	McLaughlin	2002	225.00
8173661391	Building Linux Clusters **(Book / CD-ROM)**, *360 Pages*	Spector	2002	350.00
9788184041545	Building Scalable Web Sites, *362 Pages*	Henderson	2006	325.00
8173664749	Building the Perfect PC, *360 Pages*	Thompson	2004	350.00
9788184040494	C in a Nutshell, *618 Pages*	Prinz	2005	350.00
8173666601	C Pocket Reference, *142 Pages*	Prinz	2002	100.00
9788184044423	**C# 3.0 Cookbook, 3/ed, (Throughly Revised for C# 3.0 &**			
	.NET 3.5), 902 Pages	**Hilyard**	**2008**	**650.00**
9788184044379	**C# 3.0 Design Patterns, 338 Pages**	**Bishop**	**2008**	**350.00**
9788184043846	**C# 3.0 in a Nutshell: A Desktop Quick Reference, 3/ed, 874 Pgs**	**Albahari**	**2007**	**600.00**
9788184040937	C# Cookbook, 2/ed (Updated for C# 2.0 and .NET 2.0), *1,196 Pages*	Hilyard	2006	600.00
9788184044911	**C# 3.0 Pocket Reference, 2/ed, 258 Pages**	**Albahari**	**2008**	**175.00**
8173664293	C# Essentials, 2/ed, *224 Pages*	Albahari	2002	175.00
8173665192	C# Language Pocket Reference, *132 Pages*	Drayton	2002	100.00
8173664439	C# & VB .NET Conversion Pocket Reference, *156 Pages*	Mojica	2002	75.00
9788184040364	C++ Cookbook, *604 Pages*	Stephens	2005	400.00
8173666628	C++ in a Nutshell, (Cover ISO/IEC 14882 STD) *816 Pages*	Lischner	2003	500.00
9788173667107	C++ Pocket Reference, *148 Pages*	Loudon	2003	100.00
8173662266	CDO & MAPI Programming with Visual Basic, *388 Pages*	Grundgeiger	2002	175.00
9788173660450	CGI Programming with Perl 2/ed, *476 Pages*	Gundavaram	2000	350.00
9788184042849	Cisco IOS Cookbook, 2/ed, *1,250 Pages*	Dooley	2006	850.00
8173669848	Cisco IOS in a Nutshell, 2/ed: A Desktop Quick Reference for			
	IOS on IP Network, *808 Pages*	Boney	2005	500.00
9788184047134	**CJKV Information Processing, 2/ed, 916 Pages**	**Lunde**	**2009**	**700.00**
9788173668463	Classic Shell Scripting, *568 Pages*	Robbins	2005	425.00
9788184017151	**Cloud Application Architectures:Building Applications and**			
	Infrastructure in the Cloud, 220 Pages	**Reese**	**2009**	**300.00**
8173663645	COM+ Programming with Visual Basic, *372 Pages*	Mojica	2001	225.00
8173663653	COM & .NET Component Services, *390 Pages*	Lowy	2001	250.00
9788184040197	Computer Privacy Annoyances, *218 Pages*	Tynan	2005	225.00
9788184041583	Computer Security Basics, 2/ed, *324 Pages*	Lehtinen	2006	325.00
9788173660634	Creating Effective JavaHelp, *196 Pages*	Lewis	2000	125.00
9788184040180	Creating WebSites: The Missing Manual, *559 Pages*	MacDonald	2005	400.00

	Title	Author	Year	Price
9788184047158	Creating a Web Site: The Missing Manual, 2/ed: 622 Pages	MacDonald	2009	550.00
9788184042733	CSS Cookbook, 2/ed, 552 Pages	Schmitt	2006	475.00
9788184047165	**CSS Pocket Reference:**			
	Visual Presentation for the Web, 3/ed: 184 Pgs	Meyer	2009	150.00
9788184042658	CSS Pocket Reference, 2/ed, 142 Pages	Meyer	2007	125.00
9788184042009	CSS: The Missing Manual, 494 Pages	McFarland	2006	450.00
9788184042788	CSS: The Definitive Guide, 3/ed, 550 Pages	Meyer	2006	500.00
8173667802	Database In Depth: The Relational Model for Practitioners, 250 Pages	C.J.Date	2005	250.00
8173662363	Database Nation: The Death of Privacy in the 21st Century, 336 Pages	Garfinkel	2000	235.00
9788173662898	Database Programming with JDBC & Java 2/ed, 348 Pages	Reese	2000	150.00
9788184042597	Designing Embedded Hardware, 2/ed, 406 Pages	Catsoulis	2005	275.00
9788173662423	Developing Bio-informatics Computer Skills, 504 Pages	Gibas	2001	225.00
8173669473	Developing Feeds with RSS and Atom, 280 Pages	Hammersley	2005	300.00
9788184040111	Digital Identity, 266 Pages	Windley	2005	275.00
8173665672	DNS & BIND Cookbook, 248 Pages	Liu	2002	250.00
9788184041965	DNS & BIND (Covers BIND 9.3), 5/ed, 654 Pages	Albitz	2006	550.00
8173663765	DNS on Windows 2000, 2/ed, 376 Pages	Larson	2001	275.00
9788184045567	**Dojo: The Definitive Guide, 502 Pages**	**Russell**	**2008**	**400.00**
9788184041200	Dreamweaver 8 Design and Construction, 330 Pages	Campbell	2006	375.00
9788184041033	Dreamweaver 8: The Missing Manual, 964 Pages	David	2005	600.00
8184046516519	**Dreamweaver CS4: The Missing Manual, 1,104 Pages**	**McFarland**	**2008**	**850.00**
8173662991	Dreamweaver MX: The Missing Manual, 750 Pages	McFarland	2003	600.00
9788184042771	Dynamic HTML: The Definitive Reference, 3/ed, 1,336 Pages	Goodman	2006	800.00
9788173669019	Eclipse (Coverage of 3.0), 344 Pages	Holzner	2004	325.00
9788173669309	Eclipse Cookbook (Cover 3.0), 372 Pages	Holzner	2004	350.00
8173669945	Eclipse IDE Pocket Guide, 140 Pages	Burnette	2005	125.00
8173663017	Effective awk Programming, 3/ed, 454 Pages	Robbins	2001	325.00
9788184041194	Enterprise JavaBeans 3.0, 5/ed, 774 Pages	Monson-Haefel	2006	500.00
9788184046137	**Enterprise Rails, 366 Pages**	**Chak**	**2008**	**350.00**
9788173668166	Enterprise Service Architecture - O'Reilly SAP Series, 236 Pages	Woods	2003	225.00
8173666784	Enterprise Service Bus, 284 Pages	Chappell	2004	300.00
9788184041446	Enterprise SOA, 466 Pages	Woods	2005	450.00
9788173669316	Essential ActionScript 2.0, 528 Pages	Moock	2004	400.00
9788184043662	**Essential ActionScript 3.0, 962 Pages**	**Moock**	**2007**	**600.00**
9788184040104	Essential Business Process Modeling, 362 Pages	Havey	2005	350.00
9788184042757	Essential CVS, 2/ed, 442 Pages	Vesperman	2006	425.00
9788184040920	Essential Microsoft Operation Manager, 400 Pages	Fox	2006	350.00
9788184040241	Essential PHP Security, 310 Pages	Shiflett	2005	125.00
9788184045437	**Essentail SharePoint 2007, 2/ed, 462 Pages**	**Webb**	**2008**	**475.00**
9788184042825	Essentail SNMP, 2/ed, 480 Pages	Mauro	2005	400.00
9788184045277	**Essential SQLAlchemy, 242 Pages**	**Copeland**	**2008**	**275.00**
817366529X	Essential System Administration, 3/ed, 1,178 Pages	Frisch	2002	525.00
8173666644	Essential System Administration Pocket Reference, 152 Pages	Frisch	2002	125.00
9788173660252	Essential Windows NT System Administration, 488 Pages	Frisch	1998	225.00
8173662495	Ethernet: The Definitive Guide, 528 Pages	Spurgeon	2000	300.00
9788173669613	Excel 2003 Personal Trainer (Book / CD-ROM),			
	(2 Color book) 490 Pgs	CustomGuide	2004	550.00
8173668259	Excel 2003 Programming: A Developer's Notebook, 330 Pages	Webb	2004	325.00
9788184042955	Excel 2003 for Starters: The Missing Manual, 408 Pages	MacDonald	2005	275.00
9788184042955	**Excel 2007 For Starters: The Missing Manual, 364 Pages**	**MacDonald**	**2007**	**350.00**
9788184044058	**Excel 2007 Pocket Guide, 2/ed, 180 Pages**	**Frye**	**2007**	**125.00**
9788184042559	Excel 2007: The Missing Manual, 870 Pages	MacDonald	2006	550.00
9788184043518	**Excel Hacks, 2/ed, Tips & Tools for Streamlining Your**			
	Spreadsheets, 428 Pages	**David**	**2007**	**400.00**
9788184040845	Excel Scientific and Engineering Cookbook, 442 Pages	Bourg	2006	400.00
8173665257	Exploring the JDS Linux Desktop (Book / CD-ROM), 418 Pages	Adelstein	2004	400.00
9788184042177	Fedora Linux, 672 Pages	Tyler	2006	500.00
9788184041361	Flash 8 Cookbook, 548 Pages	Lott	2006	400.00
9788184041040	Flash 8 Project for Learning Animation and			
	Interactivity (Book / CD-ROM), 372 Pages	Shupe	2006	400.00
9788184043488	Flash CS3 the Missing Manual, 542 Pages	Veer	2007	500.00

ISBN	Title	Author	Year	Price
8184046506502	Flash CS4: The Missing Manual, *768 Pages*	Grover	2008	650.00
8173667470	Flash Hacks: 100 Industrial Strength Tips & Tools, *504 Pages*	Bhangal	2004	400.00
8173668590	Flash Out of the Box: A User-Centric Beginner's Guide to Flash **(Book / CD-ROM)**, *264 Pages*	Hoekman	2004	300.00
8173667314	Flash Remoting MX: The Definitive Guide, *652 Pages*	Muck	2003	550.00
9788184045246	Flex 3 Cookbook, *798 Pages*	Noble	2008	600.00
9788184040500	FrontPage 2003: The Missing Manual, *446 Pages*	Mantaro	2005	400.00
817366868X	GDB Pocket Reference, *78 Pages*	Robbins	2005	75.00
9788184045284	*Getting Started with Flex 3: An Adobe Developer Library Pocket Guide, 162 Pages*	Herrington	2008	125.00
9788184040852	Google Advertising Tools, *366 Pages*	Davis	2006	375.00
9788184045079	Google Apps Hacks, *396 Pages*	Lenssen	2008	525.00
9788184044942	Google Hacks, 3/ed, Tips & Tools for Finding and Using the World's Information, *558 Pages*	Dornfest	2008	400.00
9788184040876	Google Maps Hacks: Tips & Tools for Geographic Searching & Remixing, *366 Pages*	Gibson	2006	350.00
8173667136	Google Pocket Guide, *144 Pages*	Calishain	2003	125.00
9788184042856	Google: The Missing Manual, 2/ed, *478 Pages*	Milstein	2006	425.00
9788184046915	Grep Pocket Reference, *98 Pages*	Bambenek	2009	125.00
8173668216	Hardcore Java, *354 Pages*	Simmons	2004	300.00
8173663424	Hardening Cisco Routers, *196 Pages*	Akin	2002	150.00
8173668213	Hardware Hacking Projects for Geeks, *358 Pages*	Fullam	2004	350.00
9788184045024	Harnessing Hibernate, *396 Pages*	Elliott	2008	400.00
9788184045819	Head First Ajax: A Brain-Friendly Guide, *544 Pages*	Riordan	2008	450.00
9788184045695	Head First Algebra: A Brain-Friendly Guide, *576 Pages*	Pilone	2009	450.00
9788184044195	Head First C# (Brain-Friendly Guides), *794 Pages*	Stellman	2007	550.00
9788173664663	Head First Design Patterns, *688 Pages*	Sierra	2004	500.00
9788173665264	Head First EJB: Passing the Sun Certified Business Component Developer Exam, *744 Pages*	Sierra	2003	450.00
9788184040821	Head First HTML with CSS & XHTML, *694 Pages*	Freeman	2005	450.00
9788173666025	Head First Java: Your Brain on Java - A Learner's Guide, 2nd Edition (Cover Java 5.0), *730 Pages*	Sierra	2005	450.00
9788184044362	Head First JavaScript: A Brain-Friendly Guide, *666 Pages*	Morrison	2008	500.00
9788184042214	Head First Object - Oriented Analysis & Design, *648 Pages*	McLaughlin	2006	425.00
9788184040418	Head First PMP, *712 Pages*	Greene	2007	550.00
9788184046571	Head First Rails: A learner's companion to Ruby on Rails, *478 Pgs*	Griffiths	2009	425.00
9788184046588	Head First PHP & MySQL : A Brain-Friendly Guide, *828 Pages*	Beighley	2009	500.00
9788184045994	Head First Physics: A Learner's Companion to Mechanics and Practical Physics, *956 Pages*	Lang	2008	525.00
9788184044973	Head First Servlets & JSP, 2/ed (COVER J2EE 1.5): Passing the Sun Certified Web Component Developer Exam, *948 Pages*	Basham	2008	650.00
9788184044508	Head First Software Development, *512 Pages*	Pilone	2008	425.00
9788184043686	Head First SQL: Your Brain on SQL -- A Learner's Guide, *624 Pages*	Beighley	2007	500.00
9788184045826	Head First Statistics: A Brain-Friendly Guide, *732 Pages*	Griffiths	2008	425.00
9788184046601	Head First Web Design: A Brain-Friendly Guide, *512 Pages*	Watrall	2009	400.00
9788184041057	Head Rush Ajax, *464 Pages*	McLaughlin	2006	375.00
9788173669347	Hibernate: A Developer's Notebook, *190 Pages*	Elliott	2004	225.00
8173669260	High Performance Linux Cluster with OSCAR, Rocks, OpenMosix, and MPI, *380 Pages*	Sloan	2004	350.00
8173669023	High Performance MySQL: Optimization, Backups, Replication & Load Balancing, *304 Pages*	Zawodny	2004	300.00
9788184047189	High Performance MySQL: Optimization, Backups, Replication 2/ed, *724 Pages*	Schwartz	2009	625.00
9788184043808	High Performance Web Sites: Essential Knowledge for Front-End Engineers, *184 Pages*	Souders	2007	200.00
8173663165	Home Hacking Projects for Geeks, *346 Pages*	Faulkner	2004	325.00
8173669449	Home Networking Annoyances: How to Fix the Most Annoying Things About Your Home Network, *234 Pages*	Ivens	2005	250.00
9788184040203	Home Networking: The Missing Manual, *263 Pages*	Lowe	2005	275.00
9788184042146	HTML & XHTML the Definitive Guide, 6/ed, *692 Pages*	Musciano	2006	500.00
9788184042696	HTML & XHTML Pocket Reference, 3/ed, *118 Pages*	Robbins	2006	125.00

ISBN	Title	Author	Year	Price
9788184042917	Information Architecture for The World Wide Web, 3/ed, 540 Pages	Morville	2006	500.00
9788184040388	Integrating Excel and Access, 232 Pages	Schmalz	2005	250.00
9788184043617	**Intel Threading Building Blocks Out fitting C++ for Multi-Core Processor Parallelism, 348 Pages**	**Reinders**	**2007**	**350.00**
9788184045635	**Intellectual Property and Open Source: A Practical Guide to Protecting Code, 406 Pages**	**Lindberg**	**2008**	**450.00**
9788184040999	Intermediate Perl, 290 Pages	Schwartz	2006	300.00
8173669414	Internet Annoyances: How to Fix the Most Annoying Things about Going Online, 266 Pages	Gralla	2005	250.00
8173661057	Internet Core Protocols: The Definitive Guide (Book / CD-ROM), 476 Pgs	Hall	2000	375.00
9788184040159	Internet Forensics, 250 Pages	Jones	2005	275.00
9788184041811	The Internet: The Missing Manual, 466 Pages	Biersdorfer	2006	350.00
9788173663376	IP Routing, 244 Pages	Malhotra	2002	250.00
978184046922	**iPhone SDK Application Development, 408 Pages**	**Zdziarski**	**2009**	**500.00**
9788184042818	IPv6 Essentials, 2/ed, 450 Pages	Hagen	2006	450.00
8173663025	IPv6 Network Administration, 316 Pages	Murphy	2005	325.00
8173667469	IRC Hack: 100 Industrial-Strength Tips & Tools, 442 Pages	Mutton	2004	400.00
9788173667374	J2EE Design Patterns, 390 Pages	Crawford	2003	400.00
8173669295	Jakarta Commons Cookbook, 412 Pages	O'Brien	2004	375.00
9788173669484	Jakarta Struts Cookbook, 536 Pages	Siggelkow	2005	400.00
8173667144	Jakarta Struts Pocket Reference, 142 Pages	Cavaness	2003	125.00
8173664471	Java & SOAP, 286 Pages	Englander	2002	275.00
8173664498	Java & XML Data Binding, 224 Pages	McLaughlin	2002	225.00
9788184043068	Java & XML, 3/ed, 496 Pages	McLaughlin	2006	450.00
8173663793	Java & XSLT, 534 Pages	Burke	2001	350.00
8173668477	Java 1.5 Tiger: A Developer's Notebook, 210 Pages	McLaughlin	2004	175.00
8173669368	Java Cookbook (Coverage of 1.5), 2/ed, 872 Pages	Darwin	2004	600.00
8173666679	Java Data Objects, 568 Pages	Jordan	2003	350.00
8173666660	Java Database Best Practices, 304 Pages	Eckstein	2003	275.00
9788173665776	Java Enterprise Best Practices, 296 Pages	Eckstein	2002	275.00
9788184042870	Java Enterprise in a Nutshell, 3/ed, 906 Pages	Farley	2005	600.00
9788173668630	Java Examples in a Nutshell: A Tutorial Companion to Java in a Nutshell, 3/ed, 728 Pages	Flanagan	2004	400.00
8173666687	Java Extreme Programming Cookbook, 296 Pages	Burke	2003	225.00
9788184042160	Java Generics and Collections, 308 Pages	Naftalin	2006	350.00
9788184042665	Java in a Nutshell, 5/ed, 1,266 Pages	Flanagan	2005	650.00
9788184041187	Java I/O, 2/ed, 740 Pages	Harold	2006	550.00
8173664404	Java Management Extensions, 318 Pages	Perry	2002	275.00
8173663211	Java Message Service, 300 Pages	Monson-Haefel	2000	225.00
9788173663536	Java Network Programming, 3/ed, 770 Pages	Harold	2004	500.00
8173665117	Java NIO, 308 Pages	Hitchens	2002	275.00
9788173665783	Java Performance Tuning, 2/ed, 600 Pages	Shirazi	2003	450.00
9788184044881	**Java Pocket Guide, 208 Pages**	**Liguori**	**2008**	**150.00**
9788184045031	**Java Power Tools, 926 Pages**	**Smart**	**2008**	**775.00**
8173663904	Java Programming with Oracle JDBC, 504 Pages	Bales	2001	300.00
9788173663819	Java RMI, 578 Pages	Grosso	2001	400.00
8173664129	Java Security, 2/ed, 624 Pages	Oaks	2001	500.00
9788173668227	Java Servlet & JSP Cookbook, 756 Pages	Perry	2004	500.00
9788184047011	**JavaSOA Cookbook, 756 Pages**	**Hewitt**	**2009**	**600.00**
8173662851	Java Servlet Programming 2/ed, 786 Pages	Hunter	2001	500.00
9788173665684	Java Swing, 2/ed, 1,288 Pages	Loy	2002	750.00
9788173665929	Java Threads (Covers J2SE 5.0), 3/ed, 368 Pages	Oaks	2004	400.00
9788173663444	Java Web Services, 286 Pages	Chappell	2002	300.00
9788184047196	**Java Web Services: Up and Running, 332 Pages**	**Kalin**	**2009**	**325.00**
8173666695	Java Web Services in a Nutshell: A Desktop Quick Reference (Covers J2EE 1.4 & JWSDP), 696 Pages	Topley	2003	500.00
9788184045451	**JavaScript and DHTML Cookbook, 2/ed, 620 Pages**	**Goodman**	**2008**	**475.00**
9788184045222	**JavaScript: The Good Parts, 186 Pages**	**Crockford**	**2008**	**200.00**
9788184041941	JavaScript: The Definitive Guide, 5/ed, 1,032 Pages	Flanagan	2006	750.00
9788184045659	**JavaScript: The Missing Manual, 560 Pages**	**McFarland**	**2008**	**450.00**
9788173669033	JavaServer Faces, 614 Pages	Bergsten	2004	450.00

ISBN	Title	Author	Year	Price
8173663831	JavaServer Pages Pocket Reference, *96 Pages*	Bergsten	2001	65.00
9788173665301	JavaServer Pages (Covers JSP 2.0 & JSTL 1.1), 3/ed, *762 Pages*	Bergsten	2003	550.00
8173669465	JBoss: A Developer's Notebook, *182 Pages*	Richards	2005	225.00
9788184040173	JBoss at Work: A Practical Guide, *318 Pages*	Marrs	2005	350.00
9788173666711	JDBC Pocket Reference, *160 Pages*	Bales	2003	100.00
9788173668609	JUnit Pocket Guide, *100 Pages*	Beck	2004	100.00
9788184041163	JUNOS Cookbook, *682 Pages*	Garrett	2006	450.00
9788184044997	**JUNOS Enterprise Routing, *828 Pages***	**Marschke**	**2008**	**800.00**
8184046426427	**JRuby Cookbook, *238 Pages***	**Edelson**	**2008**	**300.00**
817366515X	JXTA in a Nutshell: A Desktop Quick Reference, *422 Pages*	Oaks	2002	225.00
8173665605	Kerberos: The Definitive Guide, *280 Pages*	Garman	2003	275.00
8173669724	Killer Game Programming in Java, *986 Pages*	Davison	2005	675.00
9788184040265	Knoppix Pocket Reference, *104 Pages*	Rankin	2005	100.00
9788173666728	LDAP System Administration, *318 Pages*	Carter	2003	400.00
9788184040456	**Learning ASP.NET 2.0 with AJAX: A Practical Hands-on Guide, *536 Pgs***	**Liberty**	**2007**	**400.00**
9788184045666	**Learning ASP.NET 3.5, 2nd Edition ((New for Visual Studio 2008), *624 Pages***	**Liberty**	**2008**	**400.00**
9788184042863	Learning C# 2005, 2/ed, *566 Pages*	Liberty	2006	450.00
8184046466465	**Learning C# 3.0, *708 Pages***	**Liberty**	**2008**	**450.00**
8173669635	Learning GNU Emacs, 3/ed, *544 Pages*	Cameron	2004	450.00
9788184040333	Learning Java,3/ed (Book / CD-ROM) (Cover J2SE 5.0), *986 Pages*	Niemeyer	2005	650.00
9788184042153	Learning JavaScript (Covers Ajax & Dcom), *368 Pages*	Powers	2006	350.00
9788184047202	**Learning JavaScript 2/ed, *412 Pages***	**Powers**	**2009**	**400.00**
9788184042672	Learning MySQL, *632 Pages*	Tahaghoghi	2006	525.00
9788184045970	**Learning OpenCV: Computer Vision with the OpenCV Library, *592 Pages***	**Dr. Bradski**	**2008**	**500.00**
8173663912	Learning Oracle PL/SQL (Covers Oracle9i), *452 Pages*	Pribyl	2001	325.00
9788184040043	Learning Perl 4/ed, *316 Pages*	Schwartz	2005	300.00
9788184044263	**Learning Perl, 5/ed (Covers Perl 5.10), *364 Pages***	**Schwartz**	**2008**	**325.00**
9788184043716	**Learning PHP & MySQL, 2/ed: Step-by-Step Guide to Creating Database-Driven Web Sites, *444 Pages***	**Davis**	**2007**	**400.00**
9788173667329	Learning PHP 5, *378 Pages*	Sklar	2004	350.00
9788184045383	**Learning Python, 3/ed, *762 Pages***	**Lutz**	**2008**	**500.00**
8184046456458	Learning Rails, *458 Pages*	St. Laurent	2008	500.00
9788184043341	**Learning Ruby, *272 Pages***	**Fitzgerald**	**2007**	**300.00**
9788184040128	Learning SQL, *318 Pages*	Beaulieu	2005	200.00
9788184043044	**Learning SQL 2/ed, *352 Pages***	**Beaulieu**	**2009**	**325.00**
8173668051	Learning SQL on SQL Server 2005, *342 Pages*	Bagui	2006	350.00
9788173664441	Learning the Bash Shell, 3/ed, *362 Pages*	Newham	2005	375.00
9788173664236	Learning the Korn Shell, 2/ed, *438 Pages*	Rosenblett	2002	325.00
9788173660160	Learning the UNIX Operating System, 5/ed, *174 Pages*	Peek	2001	125.00
9788184045840	Learning the vi Editor 6/ed, *352 Pages*	Lamb	1998	250.00
9788184045840	**Learning the vi and Vim Editors, 7th Edition; *508 Pages***	**Robbins**	**2008**	**400.00**
9788184042689	Learning UML 2.0, *300 Pages*	Miles	2006	275.00
817366563X	Learning Visual Basic .NET, *326 Pages*	Liberty	2002	250.00
9788184043495	**Learning WCF, *624 Pages***	**Bustamante**	**2007**	**500.00**
8173669422	Learning Windows Server 2003, *682 Pages*	Hassell	2006	525.00
8184046476472	**Learning XNA 3.0: XNA 3.0 Game Development for the PC, Xbox 360, and Zune, *506 Pages***	**Reed**	**2008**	**500.00**
9788173660627	lex & yacc 2/ed, *392 Pages*	Levine	1992	225.00
9788184049904	**LINQ Pocket Reference, *188 Pages***	**Albahari**	**2008**	**150.00**
9788184041439	Linux Annoyances for Geeks, *516 Pages*	Jang	2006	400.00
8173668442	Linux Cookbook, *590 Pages*	Schroder	2004	450.00
9788184040166	Linux Desktop Pocket Guide, *202 Pages*	Brickner	2005	150.00
9788173668494	Linux Device Drivers (Covers Version 2.6.10 Linux Kernel), 3/ed, *646 Pgs*	Rubini	2005	450.00
8173669627	Linux in a Nutshell, 5/ed: A Desktop Quick Reference, *954 Pages*	Siever	2005	500.00
8173669457	Linux in a Windows World, *504 Pages*	Smith	2005	450.00
8173668507	Linux iptables Pocket Reference, *106 Pages*	Purdy	2004	100.00
9788184043525	Linux Kernel In A Nutshell, *216 Pages*	Kroah	2006	225.00
9788184040319	Linux Multimedia Hacks, *342 Pages*	Rankin	2005	350.00

ISBN	Title	Author	Year	Price
8173662541	Linux Network Administrator's Guide, 2/ed, *510 Pages*	Kirch	2000	400.00
8173664544	Linux Network Administrator's Guide, 3/ed, *372 Pages*	Kirch	2005	350.00
9788184024218	**Linux Networking Cookbook, *654 Pages***	**Schroder**	**2007**	**500.00**
9788173668647	Linux Pocket Guide, *212 Pages*	Barrett	2004	150.00
8173667187	Linux Security Cookbook, *340 Pages*	Barrett	2003	325.00
817366675X	Linux Server Hacks: 100 Industrial - Strength Tips & Tools, *240 Pgs*	Flickenger	2003	225.00
9788184040517	Linux Server Hacks: Volume 2, *490 Pages*	Hagen	2005	400.00
9788184042887	Linux Server Security, *556 Pages*	Bauer	2005	450.00
9788184043105	**Linux System Administration, *310 Pages***	**Adelstein**	**2007**	**300.00**
9788184043815	**Linux System Programming: Talking Directly to the Kernel and C Library, *404 Pages***	**Love**	**2007**	**375.00**
8173668434	Linux Unwired, *322 Pages*	Weeks	2004	300.00
9788184041781	LPI Linux Certification in a Nutshell, 2/ed, *996 Pages*	Pritchard	2006	650.00
817366465X	Managing & Using MySQL, 2/ed, *448 Pages*	Reese	2002	325.00
9788173660276	Managing IP Networks with Cisco Routers, *352 Pages*	Ballew	1997	200.00
8173669519	Managing Projects with GNU Make, 3/ed, *310 Pages*	Mecklenburg	2004	325.00
8173665230	Managing RAID on Linux, *268 Pages*	Vadala	2002	275.00
8173668655	Managing Security with Snort & IDS Tools, *296 Pages*	Cox Ph.D.	2004	300.00
9788184047028	**Masterminds of Programming, *510 Pages***	**Biancuzzi**	**2009**	**450.00**
8173662800	Managing the Windows 2000 Registry, *564 Pages*	Robicheaux	2000	325.00
9788173661167	Mastering Algorithms with C (**Book / DISK**), *572 Pages*	Loudon	1999	400.00
8173664455	Mastering FreeBSD and OpenBSD Security, *472 Pages*	Korff	2005	425.00
9788173664618	Mastering Oracle SQL (Covers Oracle Database10g), 2/ed, *504 Pages*	Mishra	2004	400.00
9788184043648	**Mastering Perl, *458 Pages***	**foy**	**2007**	**350.00**
9788173666766	Mastering Perl for Bioinformatics, *406 Pages*	Tisdall	2003	300.00
9788184043013	Mastering Regular Expressions, 3/ed, *556 Pages*	Friedl	2006	450.00
8173665702	Mastering Visual Studio .NET 2003, *420 Pages*	Flanders	2003	375.00
8173667918	Maven: A Developer's Notebook, *232 Pages*	Massol	2005	250.00
9788184045987	**Maven: The Definitive Guide, *484 Pages***	**Sonatype**	**2008**	**450.00**
9788184042184	MCSE Core Elective Exams in a Nutshell, *604 Pages*	Bhardwaj	2006	500.00
9788184041552	MCSE Core Required Exams in a Nutshell, 3/ed, *750 Pages*	Stanek	2006	450.00
9788184043730	**Microsoft Project 2007: The Missing Manual, *714 Pages***	**Biafore**	**2007**	**500.00**
9788184040524	Monad, *218 Pages*	Oakley	2005	225.00
8173667497	Mono: A Developer's Notebook, *312 Pages*	Dumbill	2004	325.00
9788184042801	MySQL Cookbook, 2/ed, *990 Pages*	DuBois	2006	750.00
817366806X	MySQL in a Nutshell, *358 Pages*	Dyer	2005	325.00
9788184045444	**MySQL Pocket Reference, 2/ed *148 Pages***	**Reese**	**2008**	**125.00**
9788184041408	MySQL Stored Procedure Programming, *650 Pages*	Harrison	2006	450.00
8173665249	NetBeans: The Definitive Guide, *662 Pages*	Boudreau	2002	500.00
8173668809	Network Security Assessment, *398 Pages*	McNab	2004	400.00
9788184044256	**Network Security Assessment: Know Your Network, 2/ed, *520 Pgs***	**McNab**	**2007**	**450.00**
9788184042740	Network Security Hacks, 2/ed, *492 Pages*	Lockhart	2006	425.00
8173668396	Network Security Tools: Writing, Hacking, and Modifying Security Tools , *350 Pages*	Dhanjani	2005	350.00
8173663688	Network Troubleshooting Tools, *370 Pages*	Sloan	2005	250.00
9788184043532	**Network Warrior, *614 Pages***	**Donahue**	**2007**	**450.00**
8173667926	Nokia Smartphone Hacks: Tips & Tools for Your Smallest Computer, *418 Pages*	Yuan	2005	400.00
8173667845	NUnit Pocket Reference, *100 Pages*	Hamilton	2004	100.00
8173668264	Office 2003 XML, *596 Pages*	Lenz	2004	450.00
9788184043303	**Office 2007 the Missing Manual, *890 Pages***	**Grover**	**2007**	**550.00**
8173667721	Open Source for the Enterprise, *246 Pages*	Woods	2005	250.00
9788184040296	Open Sources 2.0, *488 Pages*	DiBona	2005	425.00
8173667519	OpenOffice.org Writer (**Book / CD-ROM**), *234 Pages*	Weber	2004	250.00
8173667403	Optimizing Oracle Performance, *426 Pages*	Milsap	2003	375.00
8173669287	Oracle Applications Server 10g Essentials, *292 Pages*	Greenwald	2004	275.00
8173661170	Oracle Built-in Packages (**Book / DISK**), *956 Pages*	Feuerstein	1998	475.00
8173667071	Oracle Data Dictionary Pocket Reference, *150 Pages*	Kreines	2003	125.00
9788173660672	Oracle Database Administration: The Essential Reference, *552 Pages*	Kreines	1999	325.00
817366417X	Oracle DBA Checklist Pocket Reference, *88 Pages*	RevealNet	2001	65.00
9788184040005	Oracle DBA Pocket Guide, *164 Pages*	Kreines	2005	125.00

ISBN	Title	Author	Year	Price
9788173660689	Oracle Distributed Systems (Book / DISK), 552 Pages	Dye	2000	325.00
9788184044201	**Oracle Essentials: Oracle Database 11g, 4/ed, 422 Pages**	**Greenwald**	**2007**	**400.00**
817366580X	Oracle in a Nutshell: A Desktop Quick Reference, 934 Pages	Greenwald	2002	600.00
8173664560	Oracle Initialization Parameters Pocket Reference (Oracle Database 10g), 128 Pages	Kreines	2004	125.00
9788184045413	**Oracle PL/SQL Best Practices, 2/ed, 308 Pages**	**Feuerstein**	**2008**	**325.00**
8173661189	Oracle PL/SQL Built-ins Pocket Reference, 78 Pages	Feuerstein	1998	60.00
9788184040357	Oracle PL/SQL for DBAs: Security, Scheduling, Performance & More Includes Oracle Database 10g, 466 Pages	Feuerstein	2005	425.00
9788184045420	**Oracle PL/SQL Language Pocket Reference, 4/ed, 194 Pages**	**Feuerstein**	**2008**	**125.00**
9788184040487	Oracle PL/SQL Programming, 4/ed, 1,210 Pages	Feuerstein	2005	600.00
8173662401	Oracle PL/SQL Programming: A Developer's Workbook, 576 Pages	Feuerstein	2000	300.00
8173661197	Oracle PL/SQL Programming: Guide to Oracle8i Features (Book / DISK), 264 Pages	Feuerstein	1999	235.00
8173668116	Oracle Regular Expression Pocket Reference, 74 Pages	Burcham	2003	75.00
817366120 0	Oracle SAP Administration, 208 Pages	Burleson	1999	175.00
9788173660290	Oracle Scripts (Book / CD-ROM), 208 Pages	Lomansky	1998	250.00
9788173660719	Oracle Security, 448 Pages	Theriault	1998	220.00
8173663637	Oracle SQL* Loader: The Definitive Guide, 278 Pages	Gennick	2001	175.00
8173669333	Oracle SQL*Plus Pocket Reference, 3/ed, 160 Pages	Gennick	2004	125.00
8173666067	Oracle SQL*Plus: The Definitive Guide, 2/ed, 592 Pages	Gennick	2004	400.00
8173662916	Oracle SQL: The Essential Reference, 424 Pages	Kreines	2000	200.00
8173661847	Oracle Utilities Pocket Reference, 136 Pages	Mishra	2003	100.00
8173661219	Oracle Web Applications: PL/SQL Developer's Intro, 264 Pages	Odewahn	1999	180.00
9788173660283	Oracle8 Design Tips, 136 Pages	Ensor	1997	120.00
9788184042528	PC Annoyances, 2/ed :How To Fix The Most Annoying Things About Your Personal Compter, Wind & More, 268 Pages	Bass	2005	300.00
8173667152	PC Hacks: 100 Industrial-Strength Tips & Tools, 316 Pages	Aspinwall	2004	300.00
8173669732	PC Hardware Annoyances: How to Fix the Most ANNOYING Things About Your Computer Hardware, 276 Pages	Bigelow	2004	275.00
9788173665325	PC Hardware in a Nutshell: A Desktop Quick Reference, 3/ed, 848 Pgs	Thompson	2003	325.00
8173668272	PC Pest Control, 296 Pages	Gralla	2005	300.00
9788184041392	PC's: The Missing Manual, 612 Pages	Rathbone	2005	450.00
8173667128	PDF Hacks: 100 Industrial-Strength Tips & Tools, 308 Pages	Steward	2004	300.00
8173664463	Perl & XML, 224 Pages	Ray	2002	175.00
8173661073	Perl 5 Pocket Reference, 3/ed, 96 Pages	Vromans	2001	70.00
9788184042764	Perl 6 and Parrot Essentials, 2/ed, 304 Pages	Randal	2004	325.00
8173668280	Perl Best Practices, 554 Pages	Conway	2005	425.00
9788173667336	Perl Cookbook, 2/ed, 976 Pages	Christiansen	2003	675.00
9788184041385	Perl Hacks, 310 Pages	Chromatic	2006	325.00
8173668043	Perl Template Toolkit, 600 Pages	Chamberlain	2003	525.00
8173668361	Perl Testing: A Developer's Notebook, 212 Pages	Langworth	2005	225.00
9788184043006	PHP Cookbook, 2/ed, 842 Pages	Sklar	2006	550.00
9788184040814	PHP Hacks: Tips & Tools for Creating Dynamic Web Sites, 468 Pgs	Herrington	2005	400.00
9788184040234	PHP in a Nutshell, 370 Pages	Hudson	2005	325.00
9788184040258	PHPUnit Pocket Guide, 88 Pages	Bergmann	2005	100.00
817366871X	Postfix: The Definitive Guide, 288 Pages	Dent	2003	275.00
8173669805	Powerpoint 2003 Personal Trainer (Book / CD-ROM), (2 Color book) 242 Pages	CustomGuide	2004	425.00
9788184042948	**PowerPoint 2007 For Starters: The Missing Manual, 325 Pages**	**Vander**	**2007**	**325.00**
9788184042566	Powerpoint 2007: The Missing Manual, 502 Pages	Veer	2006	450.00
9788173660306	Practical C Programming 3/ed, 456 Pages	Oualline	1997	225.00
8173668822	Practical C++ Programming, 2/ed, 582 Pages	Oualline	2002	225.00
9788184040050	Practical Development Environments, 340 Pages	Doar	2005	325.00
9788184040326	Practical Perforce, 370 Pages	Wingerd	2005	375.00
8173663920	Practical PostgreSQL (Book / CD-ROM), 642 Pages	Command Prompt Inc.	2002	450.00
8173666830	Practical Unix & Internet Security, 3/ed, 994 Pages	Garfinkel	2003	650.00
8173664390	Practical VoIP Using VOCAL, 532 Pages	Dang	2002	450.00
9788184040098	Prefactoring, 248 Pages	Pugh	2005	250.00
9788184042108	Process Improvement Essentials, 364 Pages	Persse, PhD	2006	400.00
9788184040227	**Producing Open Sources Software, 302 Pages**	**Fogel**	**2005**	**325.00**

ISBN	Title	Author	Year	Price
9788184045581	The Productive Programmer, *238 Pages*	Ford	2008	275.00
9788184040340	Programming .NET Components, 2/ed (Covers .NET 2.0 & Visual Studio 2005), *656 Pages*	Lowy	2005	425.00
9788184045673	Programming .NET 3.5 (For Visual Studio 2008 and .Net 3.5), *492 Pgs*	Liberty	2008	400.00
8173667209	Programming .NET Security, *704 Pages*	Freeman	2003	550.00
9788173664380	Programming .NET Web Services, *500 Pages*	Ferrara	2002	375.00
8173667411	Programming .NET Windows Applications (Covers .NET 1.1, & Visual Studio .NET 2003), *1,316 Pages*	Liberty	2003	750.00
9788184045055	Programming Amazon Web Services: S3, EC2, SQS, FPS, and SimpleDB, *624 Pages*	Murty	2008	600.00
9788184043839	Programming ASP.NET AJAX: Build rich, Web 2.0-style UI with ASP.NET AJAX, *490 Pages*	Wenz	2007	400.00
9788184040975	Programming ASP.NET (Covers 2.0), 3/ed, *966 Pages*	Liberty	2005	600.00
9788184046113	Programming ASP.NET 3.5, 4/ed, *1,178 Pages*	Liberty	2008	750.00
9788184042085	Programming Atlas, *418 Pages*	Wenz	2006	375.00
9788184044386	Programming C# 3.0, 5/ed, (Cover Visual Studio 2008, LINQ, .NET 3.5 & More), *624 Pages*	Liberty	2008	525.00
9788173669651	Programming C# (Covers C# 2.0, .NET 2.0 & Visual Studio 2005), 4/ed, *680 Pages*	Liberty	2001	525.00
9788184043709	Programming Collective Intelligence: Building Smart Web 2.0 Applications, *376 Pages*	Segaran	2007	375.00
9788173660764	Programming Embedded Systems in C & C++, *198 Pages*	Barr	1999	150.00
9788184042627	Programming Embedded Systems with C and GNU Development Tools, 2/ed, *340 Pages*	Barr	2006	250.00
9788184041453	Programming Excel with VBA and .NET, *1,128 Pages*	Webb	2006	750.00
9788184047226	Programming Entity Framework, *844 Pages*	Lerman	2009	650.00
8173669694	Programming Flash Communication Server, *842 Pages*	Lesser	2005	600.00
9788184043358	Programming Flex 2, *518 Pages*	Kazoun	2007	425.00
9788184047233	Programming Flex 3, *674 Pages*	Kazonun	2009	575.00
8173661278	Programming Internet E-mail, *384 Pages*	Wood	1999	225.00
9788173668180	Programming Jakarta Struts 2/ed, *470 Pages*	Cavaness	2004	400.00
9788184040791	Programming MapPoint in .NET **(Book / CD-ROM)**, *400 Pages*	Thota	2005	350.00
9788173662652	Programming Perl 3/ed, *1,116 Pages*	Wall	2000	750.00
9788184042719	Programming PHP, 2/ed, *425 Pages*	Lerdorf	2006	425.00
9788184043792	Programming Python (Covers Python 2) **(Book / CD-ROM)**, 3/ed, *Pages*	Lutzf	2006	800.00
9788173667862	Programming SQL Server 2005, *500 Pages*	Wildermuth	2006	400.00
8173662371	Programming the Perl DBI, *372 Pages*	Descartes	2000	200.00
8173667063	Programming Visual Basic .NET 2003, 2/ed, *564 Pages*	Liberty	2003	425.00
9788184040371	Programming Visual Basic 2005, *580 Pages*	Liberty	2005	400.00
9788184045253	Programming Visual Basic 2008, *798 Pages*	Patrick	2008	550.00
9788184043051	Progamming WCF Services, *600 Pages*	L&oumlwy	2007	500.00
9788184047004	Progamming WCF Services, 2/ed, *800 Pages*	L&oumlwy	2009	600.00
8173665737	Programming Web Services with Perl, *492 Pages*	Ray	2002	400.00
8173662045	Programming Web Services with SOAP, *268 Pages*	Snell	2001	200.00
8173668175	Programming WPF (Covers Qt 3), 2/ed, *532 Pages*	Dalheimer	2002	450.00
9788184043723	Programming WPF, 2/ed, *880 Pages*	Sells	2007	675.00
9788184041507	Project 2003 Personal Trainer, **(Book / CD-ROM)**, *246 Pages*	CustomGuide	2005	300.00
9788173664793	Python Cookbook (Covers Python 2.3 & 2.4), 2/ed, *852 Pages*	Martelli	2005	600.00
9788184045833	Python for Unix and Linux System Administration, *472 Pages*	Gift	2008	450.00
9788184045406	Python in a Nutshell 2/ed, *726 Pages*	Martelli	2008	500.00
8173669708	Python Pocket Reference (Covers Python 2.4), 3/ed, *168 Pages*	Lutz	2005	125.00
8173668485	qmail, *268 Pages*	Levine	2004	275.00
9788184042962	Rail Cookbook, *600 Pages*	Orsini	2007	500.00
9788184046090	Rails: Up and Running, 2/ed, *232 Pages*	Tate	2008	300.00
9788184045956	Rails Pocket Reference, *212 Pages*	Berry	2008	150.00
8184046486489	Real World Haskell: Code You Can Believe In, *710 Pages*	O'Sullivan	2008	600.00
817366689X	Real World Web Services, *230 Pages*	Iverson	2004	225.00
9788184045857	Refactoring SQL Applications, *372 Pages*	Faroult	2008	350.00
9788184043761	Regular Expression Pocket Reference, 2/ed, *126 Pages*	Stubblebine	2007	150.00
9788184041989	The Relational Database Dictionary, *126 Pages*	Date	2006	150.00
9788184041378	Repairing and Upgrading Your PC, *462 Pages*	Thompson	2006	350.00

ISBN	Title	Author	Year	Price
9788184043327	Restful Web Services, *462 Pages*	Richardson	2007	400.00
9788184040869	RFID Essentials, *276 Pages*	Glover	2006	275.00
8173669686	RT Essentials, *228 Pages*	Vincent	2005	250.00
9788184041804	Ruby Cookbook, *920 Pages*	Carlson	2006	650.00
9788184041996	Ruby on Rails: Up and Running, *196 Pages*	Tate	2006	225.00
9788184043624	Ruby Pocket Reference, *182 Pages*	Fitzgerald	2007	150.00
9788184044928	The Ruby Programming Language (Covers Ruby 1.8 and 1.9), *460 Pages*	Flanagan	2008	400.00
9788184042726	Running Linux, *5/ed, 986 Pages*	Welsh	2005	600.00
8173667055	Samba Pocket Reference, *2/ed, 146 Pages*	Eckstein	2003	125.00
9788184044935	ScreenOS Cookbook, *854 Pages*	Brunner	2008	600.00
8173667217	Secure Coding: Principles & Practices, *200 Pages*	Graff	2003	225.00
8173667284	Secure Programming Cookbook for C and C++, *800 Pages*	Viega	2003	600.00
9788184047240	Search Engine Optimization for Flash, *294 Pages*	Perkins	2009	325.00
9788184043600	Securing Ajax Applications, *266 Pages*	Wells	2007	275.00
9788184047257	Security Monitoring, *262 Pages*	Fry	2009	300.00
8173669376	Securing Windows Server 2003, *456 Pages*	Danseglio	2004	400.00
9788184040081	Security and Usability, *748 Pages*	Cranor	2005	550.00
9788184043754	Security Power Tools, *872 Pages*	Burns	2007	650.00
817366840X	Security Warrior, *562 Pages*	Peikari	2004	500.00
9788173660788	sed & awk, *2/ed, 440 Pages*	Dougherty	1997	300.00
817366918X	SELINUX NSA's Open Source Security Enhanced Linux, *264 Pages*	McCarty	2004	275.00
817366823X	sendmail Cookbook, *418 Pages*	Hunt	2003	400.00
9788184044225	sendmail, *4/ed, 1,324 Pages*	Costales	2007	850.00
8173666865	Sequence Analysis in a Nutshell: A Guide to Common Tools and Databases (Covers EMBOSS 2.5.0), *310 Pages*	Markel	2003	275.00
9788184040449	SharePoint 2007: The Definitive Guide, *836 Pages*	Pyles	2007	600.00
9788184046144	SharePoint for Project Management, *266 Pages*	Raymond	2008	300.00
817366983X	SharePoint Office Pocket Guide, *94 Pages*	Webb	2005	100.00
817366739X	SharePoint User's Guide, *158 Pages*	IDC	2005	150.00
9788184040678	Skype Hacks: Tips & Tools for Cheap, Fun, Innovative Phone Service, *354 Pages*	Sheppard	2005	350.00
8173669503	Snort Cookbook, *296 Pages*	Orebaugh	2005	300.00
9788184043693	SOA in Practice: The Art of Distributed System Design (Theory in Practice), *358 Pages*	Josuttis	2007	375.00
8173669198	SpamAssassin (Covers 3.0), *232 Pages*	Schwartz	2004	250.00
8173668191	Spidering Hacks: 100 Industrial - Strength Tips & Tools, *436 Pages*	Hemenway	2003	350.00
9788173668371	Spring: A Developer's Notebook, *202 Pages*	Tate	2005	225.00
9788184046939	SQL and Relational Theory: How to Write Accurate SQL Code, *442 Pages*	Date	2009	350.00
9788184040685	SQL Cookbook (Cover SQL Server, PostgreSQL,Oracle, MySQL, AND DB2), *640 Pages*	Molinaro	2005	475.00
9788184042207	SQL Hacks, *424 Pages*	Cumming	2006	400.00
8173666520	SQL in a Nutshell (Covers SQL Server, DB2, MySQL, Oracle & PostgreSQL), *2/ed, 720 Pages*	Kline	2004	450.00
9788184047264	SQL IN A NUTSHELL 3/ed, *606 Pages*	Kline	2009	500.00
9788817366;7435	SQL Pocket Guide (Cover Oracle. DB2, SQL Server & MySQL), *170 Pgs*	Gennick	2006	125.00
9788173668241	SQL Tunning (Covers Oracle, DB2 & SQL Server), *356 Pages*	Tow	2003	325.00
8173668418	Squid: The Definitive Guide, *472 Pages*	Wessels	2004	450.00
9788184042795	SSH The Secure Shell: The Definitive Guide, *2/ed, 680 Pages*	Barrett	2005	525.00
9788184042634	Statistics Hacks, *380 Pages*	Frey	2006	350.00
9788184045680	Statistics in a Nutshell: A Desktop Quick Reference, *492 Pages*	Boslaugh	2008	250.00
8173668574	STL Pocket Reference, *136 Pages*	Lischner	2003	100.00
9788184045048	Subject To Change: Creating Great Products & Services for an Uncertain World: Adaptive Path on Design, *226 Pages*	Merholz	2008	300.00
9788184041798	SUSE Linux, *460 Pages*	Brown	2006	400.00
8173664811	Swing Hacks, *554 Pages*	Marinacci	2005	425.00
8173665311	Switching to VoIP, *514 Pages*	Wallingford	2005	450.00
8173669511	SWT: A Developer's Notebook, *330 Pages*	Hatton	2004	325.00
9788184040531	Talk is Cheap: Switching to Internet Telephones, *278 Pages*	Gaskin	2005	275.00
9788173660931	Tcl/Tk in a Nutshell: A Desktop Quick Reference, *480 Pages*	Raines	1999	240.00

ISBN	Title	Author	Year	Price
8173664676	TCP/IP Network Administration 3/ed, *756 Pages*	Hunt	2002	500.00
8173666512	Test Driving Linux: From Windows to Linux in 60 Seconds **(Book / CD-ROM)**, *372 Pages*	Brickner	2005	350.00
9788184040302	Time Management for System Administrators, *238 Pages*	Limoncelli	2005	250.00
8173666032	TOAD Pocket Reference for Oracle, 2/ed, *136 Pages*	McGrath	2005	125.00
9788184044041	**Tomcat: The Definitive Guide, 2/ed (Cover TOMCAT 6.0), 358 Pgs**	**Brittain**	**2007**	**400.00**
9788184046946	**The Art of Application Performance Testing, 174 Pages**	**Molyneaux**	**2009**	**200.00**
9788184046953	**The Art of Lean Software Development, 158 Pages**	**Hibbs**	**2009**	**200.00**
9788184047271	**Twitter API: Up and Running, 429 Pages**	**Makice**	**2009**	**450.00**
9788184040210	Twisted Network Programming Essentials, *210 Pages*	Fettig	2005	275.00
9788184041590	Ubuntu Hacks, *462 Pages*	Oxer	2006	350.00
9788184040029	UML 2.0 in a Nutshell, *246 Pages*	Pilone	2005	200.00
9788184042993	UML 2.0 Pocket Reference, *150 Pages*	Pilone	2006	125.00
9788184040760	Understanding Linux Network Internals, *1,074 Pages*	Benvenuti	2005	600.00
9788184043198	**Understanding MySQL Internals, 208 Pages**	**Pachey**	**2007**	**300.00**
9788184040838	Understanding the Linux Kernel (Cover Version 2.6), 3/ed, *954 Pages*	Bovet	2005	550.00
9788184041606	Unicode Explained, *692 Pages*	Korpela	2006	525.00
8184046436434	**Universal Design for Web Applications: Web Applications That Reach Everyone, 214 Pages**	**Chisholm**	**2008**	**300.00**
817366627X	Unit Test Frameworks **(Book / CD-ROM)**, *222 Pages*	Hamill	2004	225.00
9788184040609	Unix in a Nutshell, 4/ed, *992 Pages*	Robbins	2005	450.00
9788173665653	Unix Power Tools, 3/ed, *1,162 Pages*	Powers	2002	750.00
8173666202	Upgrading to PHP 5 (Covers MySQL 4.1), *358 Pages*	Trachtenberg	2004	350.00
9788173660948	Using & Managing PPP, *464 Pages*	Sun	1999	240.00
8173665842	Using Samba, 2/ed, *570 Pages*	Eckstein	2003	500.00
9788184043037	**Using Samba, 3/ed, 464 Pages**	**Carter**	**2007**	**450.00**
817366594X	VB .NET Language Pocket Reference, *160 Pages*	Roman	2002	125.00
8173661340	VBScript in a Nutshell: A Desktop Quick Reference, 2/e, *528 Pages*	Lomax	2003	400.00
8173668582	Version Control With Subversion, *332 Pages*	Collins - Sussman	2004	350.00
9788184047288	**Version Control with Subversion 2/ed, 446 Pages**	**Pilato**	**2009**	**475.00**
8173662622	vi Editor Pocket Reference, *76 Pages*	Robbins	1999	60.00
8173661340	Virtual Private Networks, 2/ed, *228 Pages*	Scott	1998	150.00
9788184042092	Visual Basic 2005 Cookbook, *754 Pages*	Craig	2006	575.00
9788184040913	Visual Basic 2005 in a Nutshell 3/ed, *766 Pages*	Patrick	2006	500.00
9788184040067	Visual Basic 2005 Jumpstart, *226 Pages*	Lee	2005	225.00
8173666164	Visual Basic 2005: A Developer's Notebook, *272 Pages*	MacDonald	2005	250.00
8173660964	Visual Basic Controls in a Nutshell, *512 Pages*	Dictor	1999	310.00
8173669740	Visual C# 2005: A Developer's Notebook, *250 Pages*	Liberty	2005	225.00
9788184040692	VOIP Hacks: Tips & Tools for Internet Telephony, *326 Pages*	Wallingford	2006	325.00
9788184045062	**Web 2.0: A Strategy Guide: Business thinking and strategies behind successful Web 2.0 implementations, 302 Pages**	**Shuen**	**2008**	**350.00**
9788173669057	Web Database Application with PHP & MySQL (Covers PEAR, PHP 5 & MySQL 4.1), 2/ed, *828 Pages*	Willaims	2004	600.00
8173663750	Web Design in a Nutshell: A Desktop Quick Reference, 2/ed, *656 Pgs*	Niederst	2001	425.00
9788184040982	Web Design in a Nutshell: A Desktop Quick Reference, 3/ed, *826 Pgs*	Niederst	2006	450.00
8173664412	Web Performance Tuning, 2/ed, *488 Pages*	Killelea	2002	350.00
8173665214	Web Privacy with P3P, *350 Pages*	Cranor	2002	300.00
8173663947	Web Security, Privacy & Commerce, 2/ed, *768 Pages*	Garfinkel	2001	500.00
9788184046151	**Web Security Testing Cookbook, 328 Pages**	**Hope**	**2008**	**350.00**
9788173663390	Web Services Essentials, *320 Pages*	Cerami	2002	200.00
8173667624	Web Site Cookbook, *262 Pages*	Addison	2006	300.00
8173669678	Web Site Measurement Hacks: Tips & Tools to Help Optimize Your Online Business, *442 Pages*	Peterson	2005	400.00
9788184045628	**Website Optimization, 408 Pages**	**King**	**2008**	**450.00**
8173663092	WebLogic 8.1: The Definitive Guide, *860 Pages*	Mountjoy	2004	650.00
8173661308	The Whole Internet: The Next Generation, *576 Pages*	Conner/Krol	1999	425.00
8173661367	Win32 API Programming with Visual Basic **(Book / CD-ROM)**, *534 Pages*	Roman	1999	400.00
8173663319	Windows 2000 Commands Pocket Reference, *122 Pages*	Frisch	2001	60.00
9788184042603	Windows Developers Power Tools, *1,322 Pages*	Avery	2006	750.00

ISBN	Title	Author	Year	Price
9788173660887	Windows NT TCP/IP Network Administration, *512 Pages*	Hunt	1999	250.00
9788184044034	**Windows PowerShell Cookbook: for Windows,** **Exchange 2007, and MOM V3,** *600 Pages*	**Holmes**	**2007**	**500.00**
9788184045239	Windows PowerShell Pocket Reference, *182 Pages*	**Holmes**	**2008**	**150.00**
9788184040777	Windows Server 2003 Security Cookbook, *522 Pages*	Danseglio	2005	475.00
9788184045000	**Windows Server 2008: The Definitive Guide,** *508 Pages*	**Hassell**	**2008**	**475.00**
8173668833	Windows Server Hacks: 100 Industrial-Strength Tips & Tools , *328 Pages*	Tulloch	2004	325.00
9788184042979	**Windows Vista For Starters: The Missing Manual,** *493 Pages*	**Pogue**	**2007**	**325.00**
9788184042986	Windows Vista In A Nutshell, *766 Pages*	Gralla	2006	500.00
9788184043075	**Windows Vista Pocket Reference,** *208 Pages*	**Gralla**	**2007**	**150.00**
9788184042139	**Windows Vista: The Definitive Guide,** *958 Pages*	**Stanek**	**2007**	**600.00**
9788184042580	Windows Vista: The Missing Manual, *860 Pages*	Pogue	2006	600.00
817366966X	Windows XP Cookbook, *690 Pages*	Allen	2005	500.00
8173667454	Windows XP Hacks: 100 Industrial-Strength Tips & Tools, *294 Pages*	Gralla	2003	350.00
8173669643	Windows XP Personal Trainer (**Book / CD-ROM**), *480 Pages*	CustomGuide	2004	550.00
8173666911	Windows XP Pocket Reference, *196 Pages*	Karp	2002	125.00
9788184043020	Wireless Hacks, 2/ed: Tips & Tools For Building, Extending & Securing Your Network 2/ed, *480 Pages*	Flickenger	2005	425.00
9788184042931	**Word 2007 For Starters: The Missing Manual,** *372 Pages*	**Grover**	**2007**	**350.00**
817366692X	Word Pocket Guide, *160 Pages*	Glenn	2003	125.00
9788173605356	Writing Excel Macros with VBA, 2/ed, *580 Pages*	Roman	2002	450.00
9788184044430	**X Power Tools,** *286 Pages*	**Tyler**	**2008**	**325.00**
9788184041422	XAML in a Nutshell, *316 Pages*	MacVittie	2006	300.00
8173666156	XML Hacks: 100 Industrial-Strength Tips & Tools, *490 Pages*	Fitzgerald	2004	425.00
9788173668456	XML in a Nutshell (Covers XML 1.1 & XInclude), 3/ed, *724 Pages*	Harold	2005	500.00
8173663343	XML Pocket Reference, 2/ed, *128 Pages*	Eckstein	2003	100.00
9788184042641	XML Pocket Reference, 3/ed, *198 Pages*	Laurent	2005	125.00
9788184047295	**XMPP: The Definitive Guide,** *324 Pages*	**Saint**	**2009**	**375.00**
9788184043181	**XQuery,** *528 Pages*	**Walmsley**	**2007**	**500.00**
9788184045574	**XSLT, 2nd Edition ((Now Covers XSLT 2.0),** *1,002 Pages*	**Tidwell**	**2008**	**650.00**
8173664900	XSLT 1.0 Pocket Reference, *188 Pages*	Lenz	2005	150.00
9788184040784	XSLT Cookbook (Cover XSLT 1.0 & 2.0, 2/ed, *786 Pages*	Mangano	2005	500.00
9788184040074	Yahoo! Hacks: Tips & Tools for Living on the Web Frontier, *504 Pages*	Bausch	2005	400.00
9788184040883	Zero Configuration Networking: The Definitive Guide, *252 Pages*	Cheshire	2005	275.00
US EDITION AVAILABLE AT INDIA SPECIAL PRICE:				
0596102364	Adobe Creative Suite 2 Workflow, *634 Pages*	Alspach	2005	1,625.00
0596006004	Adobe Encore DVD: In the Studio, *336 Pages*	Dixon	2004	1,225.00
9780596529765	**Adobe InDesign CS3 One-On-One (Book / DVD),** *560 Pages*	**McClelland**	**2007**	**US$ 44.00**
9780596529758	**Adobe Photoshop CS3 One-On-One (Book / DVD),** *544 Pages*	**McClelland**	**2007**	**US$ 40.00**
9780596101367	Building Extreme PCs, *192 Pages*	Hardwidge	2006	1,200.00
0596001088	The Cathedral & The Bazaar: Musings On Linux and Open Source by an Accidental Revolutionary, Revised & Expanded, *256 Pgs*	Raymond	2001	525.00
059600849X	Commercial Photoshop Retouching: In The Studio, *410 Pages*	Honiball	2005	1,425.00
0596008589	Creating Photomontages with Photoshop: A Designer's Notebook, *96 Pgs*	Collandre	2005	800.00
9780596100476	**The Creative Digital Darkroom,** *429 Pages*	**Eismann**	**2008**	**US$ 40.00**
9780596008031	Designing Interfaces, *352 Pages*	Tidwell	2005	1,800.00
9780596528102	**Designing Web Navigation: Optimizing the User Experience,** *456 Pgs*	**Kalbach**	**2007**	**US$ 40.00**
9780596526801	**Devices of the Soul Batting for Our Selves in an Age of** **Machines,** *302 Pages*	**Talbott**	**2007**	**US$ 18.00**
0596005474	Digital Photography: Expert Techniques (Covers Photoshop CS), *496 Pages*	Milburn	2003	1,375.00
0596006667	Digital Photography Hacks: 100 Industrial - Strength Tips & Tools, *336 Pages*	Story	2004	800.00
0596100159	Digital Photography Pocket Guide, 3/ed, *160 Pages*	Story	2005	450.00
0596008414	Digital Photography: The Missing Manual, *432 Pages*	Grover	2006	1,200.00
0596009461	Digital Video Hacks: Tips & Tools for Shooting, Editing & Sharing, *426 Pages*	Paul	2005	800.00
0596005237	Digital Video Pocket Guide, *474 Pages*	Story	2005	500.00
9780596510572	**Dynamic Learning Dreamweaver CS3 (Book / DVD),** *416 Pgs*	**Gerantabee**	**2007**	**US$ 36.00**

ISBN	Title	Author	Year	Price
9780596510589	Dynamic Learning Flash CS3 (Book / DVD), 456 Pages	Gerantabee	2007	US$ 36.00
9780596510619	Dynamic Learning: Photoshop CS3 (Book / DVD), 360 Pages	Smith	2007	US$ 36.00
9780596102425	Fonts & Encodings, 1,037 Pages	Haralambous	2007	US$ 48.00
0596002874	Free As In Freedom: Richard Stallman's Crusade for Free Software, 243 Pages	Williams	2002	750.00
9780596006624	Hackers & Painters: Big Ideas From the Computer Age, 276 Pages	Graham	2004	700.00
9780596526856	Illustrated Guide to Astronomical Wonders: From Novice to Master Observer (DIY Science), 519 Pages	Thompson	2007	US$ 24.00
0596008597	Illustrations with Photoshop: A Designer's Notebook, 96 Pages	Rodarmor	2004	775.00
0596100485	InDesign Production Cookbook, 224 Pages	Dabbs	2005	1,200.00
059600768X	Just A Geek, 296 Pages	Wheaton	2004	700.00
9780596527877	Learning ActionScript 3.0: A Beginner's Guide, 382 Pages	Shupe	2008	US$ 32.00
9780596517328	Learning Flex 3: Getting up to Speed with Rich Internet Applications (Adobe Developer Library), 304 Pages	Cole	2008	US$ 32.00
9780596527525	Learning Web Design: A Beginner's Guide to (X)HTML, StyleSheets, and Web Graphics, 3/ed, 479 Pages	Robbins	2007	US$ 36.00
9780596517717	Making Things Happen: Mastering Project Management (Theory in Practice), 408 Pages	Berkun	2008	US$ 32.00
0596007035	Mapping Hacks: Tips & Tools for Electronic Cartography, 574 Pages	Erle	2005	900.00
9780596527051	Myths of Innovation, 196 Pages	Berkun	2007	US$ 20.00
0596008600	Photo Retouching with Photoshop: A Designer's Notebook, 96 Pages	CLEC'H	2004	775.00
9780596100209	Photoshop Blending Modes Cookbook for Digital Photographers, 176 Pages	Beardsworth	2005	1,025.00
9780596515041	Photoshop CS3 Photo Effects Cookbook: 53 Easy-to-Follow Recipes for Digital Photographers, Designers, and Artists, 176 Pages	Shelbourne	2007	US$ 24.00
0596008511	Photoshop CS2 Raw: Using Adobe Camera Raw, Bridge, and Photoshop to Get the Most Out of Your Digital Camera, 206 Pages	Aaland	2006	1,075.00
9780596510527	Photoshop CS3 Raw: Get the Most Out of the Raw Format with Adobe Photoshop, Camera Raw, and Bridge, 272 Pages	Aaland	2008	US$ 28.00
0596100213	Photoshop Filter Effects Encyclopedia, 176 Pages	Pring	2005	1,050.00
0596100620	Photoshop Fine Art Effects Cookbook, 176 Pages	Beardsworth	2006	1,050.00
9780596100995	Photoshop Lightroom Adventure: Mastering Adobe's next-generation tool for digital photographers, 350 Pages	Aaland	2007	US$ 32.00
0596100221	Photoshop Photo Effects Cookbook, 176 Pages	Shelbourne	2005	1,025.00
0596100302	Photoshop Retouching Cookbook for Digital Photographers, 176 Pages	Huggins	2005	1,025.00
9780596101138	Programming Windows Presentation Foundation, 430 Pages	Sells	2005	1,100.00
9780596007195	Revolution in the Valley, 324 Pages	Hertzfeld	2004	775.00
9780596523701	Stephen Johnson on Digital Photography, 320 Pages	Johnson	2006	1,500.00
0596007337	We the Media: Grassroots Journalism by the People, for the People, 320 Pages	Gillmor	2004	775.00
0596100833	Windows Seat, 152 Pages	Kost	2006	1,600.00

- Dates & Prices of forthcoming titles are tentative and subject to change without notice.
- All Prices are in Indian Rupees.
- TITLES RELEASED AFTER January 2007 ARE MARKED IN BOLD.